Canals to Manchester

Canals to Manchester

DAVID OWEN

Manchester University Press

© DAVID OWEN 1977

Published by Manchester University Press
Oxford Road, Manchester M13 9PL

First published 1977
Reprinted in paperback 1987

British Library cataloguing in publication data

Owen, David
Canals to manchester.
1. Manchester metropolitan area – Canals – History
I. Title
386'.46'094273   HE436.M/

ISBN 0 7190 2631 8

Printed in Great Britain
by A. Wheaton & Co. Ltd, Exeter

Contents

Preface

Manchester is the centre of a complex of canals, some narrow, some wide, and one, the Ship Canal, an ocean seaway. Most of the great canal engineers from James Brindley to Leader Williams had some part in their construction. This book describes their history and the problems that beset their builders. Quotations from contemporary accounts paint a picture of the navigations in their heyday, and their appearance today is recorded both from the water and from the towpath. The book is aimed at those who find interest in canals busy or derelict and who want to know where to go to see their most notable engineering structures. Teachers with classes studying local history or communications will find it invaluable and so will ramblers and nature lovers who want to know more about the quiet waterside paths from the city centre to the green country.

I would like to record my thanks to Mr A. Hayman of the Manchester Ship Canal Company for his advice on parts of the manuscript and for allowing me to reproduce the maps on pp. 19, 34 and 35, to Mrs D. Hirst for redrawing the diagram from Dutens, to Drs F. Ratcliffe and A. J. N. W. Prag for translating German passages, to Mr F. Mullineux and Mr J. Ripley for the loan of photographs reproduced on pp. 18, 28–30, 36, 47 and 48 and p. 94 respectively, to Mr D. C. Graham for the drawings of the Ashton Canal warehouse, to Mr G. Bridge for drawing the area map, to Mr M. Alcard for the bill heading on p. 92 and to the Director of Rochdale Museum for the photograph on p. 65. Other photographs are from old books kindly copied by the John Rylands University Library and Manchester Museum or from my own camera. I am grateful to my wife, Pearl, for accompanying me throughout and for reading and criticising the manuscript.

1

Introduction

Canals were once the arteries of the country, carrying raw materials to the towns, finished·goods to the ports and food to the workmen. During the Napoleonic wars they transported troops and supplies from one end of the country to the other, and in peacetime they were the main trade routes. Today trade has left all but a few, and their purpose has changed. For pleasure, they form green fingers from busy towns to quiet countryside, they have a quality of remoteness and their buildings have a grace seldom seen today. They attract anglers, boaters, walkers and nature lovers, bird watchers and botanists. In addition they have a role never considered by their builders, for they carry water from reservoirs in the hills to industries in the thirsty towns. Manchester is fortunate in having many canals and can claim the first – the Bridgewater – and the last – the Ship Canal – to be built in England.

Manchester's importance dates back at least as far as the sixteenth century, for though the town was politically of little consequence, industrially it had already come to the fore. Tupling[45] described how the spinning and weaving of woollen cloths was carried out by smallholders in the Pennines, and of coarse linens and sacking from flax and hemp grown in low-lying west Lancashire. The products had to be sold, and Manchester was well placed as a centre for the trade. Merchants and dealers established links with London, and the town grew in size, importance and wealth. By the early seventeenth century cotton was being used, mostly brought via London from the Levant.

The chief difficulty in extending and developing trade at this period, particularly for an inland town, was that of transport. Lancashire was notorious for its bad roads in the seventeenth century,[5] and this is easy to understand. Much of the western side of the county is low-lying, the marshy surface resting on a substratum of boulder clay. Even the gritstone moors to the east are thickly covered by peat, which provided a poor foundation for the primitive roads of the time. The paved causeways were sufficiently wide for horses but not for carts, and in wet weather the tracks became morasses.

Transport at that time was either by packhorse trains, strings of horses with panniers across their backs, or waggons or carts drawn by horses. The latter could travel only in fairly dry weather, and both methods were slow. Coastal towns could rely on shipping, which could also creep up the major rivers and estuaries. Craft were developed which were specially adapted to their area. The Humber keels, with their shallow draft, their square sails, their leeboards for working to windward, came far inland in Yorkshire. The Severn trow was similarly suitable for the coast, the river and the tidal estuary, and the Thames barge had a comparable history.

Many towns were too far up the rivers or were served by rivers too small to carry craft of any size. Manchester and its south Lancashire neighbours were in this position. It is not surprising that turnpike roads and river navigations were developed around Manchester in the eighteenth century.

Even with better surfaced roads usable for longer periods of the year, communications were still restricted by the size of the conveyance, for steam-driven locomotives were still a long way off. Coal had been moved for generations by cart and by packhorse, but this was expensive and few could afford the cost. Salt was carried by packhorse, and many of the saltways can be followed by the names they left behind them. Saltersford and Salford mark the crossings of the rivers. Lime for improving the sour fields was generally too bulky and expensive to be carried far from its source. There was a great need to develop carriage by water and to bring coastal and estuary craft as far inland as possible by developing river navigations. The background history of this has been written by Willan.[48] [49]

Most rivers in the country start as hill streams with a fairly steep course, gradually levelling off as they reach the sea. Throughout the Tertiary period – roughly the last sixty million years – the sea level around our coasts was much higher than it is today, and the lowering was intermittent, with long pauses. As the sea level fell, the rivers cut back their channels, and a typical river profile consists of a series of curves, each steeper section cutting into the flatter part of the curve above. Even the smaller streams of Lancashire and Cheshire are known to have graded to sea levels two hundred and one hundred feet above the present. Almost the last event towards the end of the Pleistocene Ice Age was a rise in sea level which flooded the seaward ends of the valleys, producing tidal estuaries. In addition, the rivers themselves are held up by resistant rocks running across the channel.

Typically each river has a series of relatively deep, level reaches interspersed with shallower stretches when the slope is steeper and the flow faster, lengths where navigation is difficult. In early navigations a weir was placed across the river to raise the water level and a gate was made in the weir. This could be raised, and boats coming down could shoot through with the current. Those coming up would have to wait until the flow had slackened sufficiently for them to be drawn through. This method was often dangerous and was extremely wasteful of water. Moreover, water mills were often sited in such a position, the weir building up a head of water to drive their wheels. The raising of the gate for a boat to pass would often lower the water to such an extent that the mill was brought to a halt.

The Chinese realised that two such water gates, or flash locks, as they are also called, placed close together and impounding water between them, were suitable for boats and wasted much less water. This was the origin of the 'pound lock' used throughout today. Furthermore an artificial cut containing the pound lock could be built alongside the weir, and a single weir only was then necessary. Such pound locks could be much deeper than flash locks and fewer were needed to make the river navigable. The lock channels could be sited in such a way as to shorten the whole navigation. Lock chambers have been built of many different materials, including stone, brick, timber and even turf. Lock gates of wood, or more recently of steel, can be raised like a guillotine or swung back on hinges. The first pound locks in England were built on the Exeter canal in 1564 and at Waltham Abbey on the Lee ten years later.

River navigations were undoubtedly of the greatest importance as means of communication, allowing goods in bulk to be brought farther inland. There were, however, a number of factors which materially reduced their value. In times of drought the general level of the river could fall so low that boats would be aground for weeks at a time waiting for enough water to continue their passage. When carrying stone, sand or even coal the boatmen would often shovel some overboard to lighten their load, and this would make the bad places worse. Most of the craft sailed with a favourable breeze or were towed from the bank by men who were known as halers. In periods of flood the current could be so strong that no progress could be made and the boat was once more forced to wait until it had subsided. In addition, the river could rise so much that it was impossible to take a boat beneath the arches of some of the bridges.

The father of English canals is rightly claimed to be the third Duke of Bridgewater, for it was he who obtained the first Act for a canal in England entirely independent of rivers. There were older canals on the Continent, notably the Canal du Midi, which linked the Atlantic with the Mediterranean. It was the success of the Bridgewater that convinced industrialists throughout the country that here was the answer to the carriage of goods even in a country as hilly as England. It was also the success of the Bridgewater that brought James Brindley and his associates to the fore as canal engineers. In fact Brindley had already surveyed the routes of what were to become his Grand Cross, linking the ports of the Mersey, the Humber, the Severn and Avon and the Thames.

The canal differed from the river navigation in being independent of rivers except those used to feed it. It ran on a series of levels, stepping up by locks over the hills or running beneath them in tunnels. It crossed the valleys on long raised embankments and the rivers and roads on aqueducts. Provided that it was suitably fed with water, especially on its highest levels, it was unaffected by floods or droughts, and the water was practically still. Great care was taken to make the bed watertight during construction, and this was usually done by laying a bed of puddled clay across the entire channel and behind the side walls. Reservoirs were built in the hills, and additional water came from mines and, in some cases, from rivers and streams. Canals make delightful venues for cruising, for the boatman may look down across wide areas of countryside. Because they cross watersheds it was possible to build an interconnecting network of water roads to cover the whole country.

When the Bridgewater canal was built it was on one level except where it stepped down to the tidal Mersey. Since much of the traffic never used the locks at its western end, there was seldom a serious problem over water. When Brindley surveyed his lines across the country he realised that water would be a major problem and that he would need to drive tunnels through the hills. Canal tunnels of any length had never been built before but it was obviously less difficult to make them of smaller bore than to construct them to the full barge width. Brindley knew a great deal about the duke's navigable soughs at Worsley (see chapter 3) and about the boats that used them. He decided on the present narrow gauge, with locks approximately seventy feet by seven, and this set the pattern for a great deal of the network.

A number of wide canals were built, but they do not form a complete network. Examples in the Manchester area are the Rochdale, with locks large enough to take a pair of narrow boats side by side, the Bridgewater, with similar dimensions, and the Manchester, Bolton and Bury, whose locks are as wide but are slightly shorter. Just outside the area is the Leeds and Liverpool canal, whose locks above Wigan are all of barge width but are shorter still. Those below Wigan were lengthened to take barges and pairs of narrow boats from the Bridgewater.

The coming of canals at different periods had a marked effect on Manchester and its surrounding towns. With the opening of the Bridgewater the price of coal was reduced to less than half and it became available to many more people. In the nineteenth century steam was replacing water power to drive the machinery, and the large red-brick mills were sited along the canal side where cheap coal could be carried to their bunkers and water supplied to their boilers. Towards the end of that century the Ship Canal was opened and Manchester was put in direct communication with ports all over the world. Trafford Park, the first industrial estate in the country and the largest in Europe, was built on its south bank. The timing proved fortunate,[5] for the world depression of the last quarter of the nineteenth century was ending and the Ship Canal allowed Manchester to compete on favourable terms with its rivals.

Though coal, lime, timber, salt and other bulk materials have always been the main cargoes, canals were extremely important in other ways. As the population of towns grew, food had to be brought in growing quantities from the surrounding countryside. Aikin[1] described how early cabbages came from gardens round Warrington and carrots, peas and beans from the sandy soils of Bowdon. Potatoes came from Frodsham and Runcorn and apples from even farther afield. Milk, butter and poultry all came from outlying farms. A great deal of fish was brought from the Yorkshire coast and rather less from Lancashire. As most of these foods were perishable, speed was essential for their carriage, and the flyboat became a conspicuous feature of the canals. These vessels were usually of lighter construction and built for greater speed. They had precedence over other boats, which had to drop their towlines into the water and allow the flyboat to take the channel inside them. Drawn by relays of horses, they travelled by night as well as by day, not stopping until they reached their destination.

Another important use of canals was the carriage of passengers. Dickens and others have written descriptions of coach travel, which could be most uncomfortable on bad roads and was often very slow. Canal transport in the 'packet boats' was sometimes quicker and was certainly much easier. Head[17] described his journey on the Lancaster canal, which lay on two long levels separated by a group of eight locks. A total journey of fifty-seven miles was normally accomplished in seven hours, the finely constructed boats being towed by teams of horses at a canter, changed every four miles. The Rev. Adam Sedgwick, the great Cambridge geologist, made the journey in 1815 and carried with him the news of the battle of Waterloo to his home town of Dent. The journey was not without its moments of excitement, for slower barges might be met at bridges and corners where they had little time to give way.

Some idea of the passenger traffic in the Manchester area can be gained from the Manchester and Salford directories for the early years of the nineteenth century. For the Bridgewater canal there is the record of 'two elegant Passage-boats, Richard Hampson and James Parkinson, Masters, for passengers and luggage only' which ran from Manchester to Runcorn daily. The one left Castle Quay at eight o'clock, reached Altrincham at ten o'clock, London Bridge, near Warrington, at one o'clock, Preston Brook at three o'clock and Runcorn two hours later. Coaches met the boats at Preston Brook for Chester and London Bridge for Warrington and Liverpool. The other made the journey in the opposite direction, leaving Warrington at ten o'clock and reaching Manchester at six o'clock. No reason is given for the boat from Manchester taking an hour longer over the journey.

Similarly boats went from Leigh through Worsley to Manchester and returned the same day. The fares from Manchester to London Bridge were 2s 6d for the 'front room' and 1s 6d for the 'back room'. Those from Manchester to Worsley were 2s and 1s for these two cabins.

The Mersey and Irwell 'elegant and commodious Packet boats for passengers and their luggage' sailed daily from Manchester to Runcorn, and a 'new and commodious steam packet' met the boat and carried passengers on to Liverpool. These left Manchester at eight o'clock, reached Warrington at 1.45 and left again at two, finally reaching Runcorn at four o'clock. The boat from Runcorn left at ten and reached Manchester at six. The fares were the same as those on the Bridgewater, and the timing of the return journey was identical. It would seem that they were not in competition but that their timing was calculated to allow the journey to be completed the same day. There is little wonder that the opening of the Liverpool to Manchester railway in September 1830, cutting the time spent on the journey to an hour and a half, skimmed off the passenger traffic and spelt doom to the packet boats.

Manchester and its surroundings are particularly suitable for the study and enjoyment of canals from many different points of view. Places can be chosen for a sixth-form group, for an extra-mural class or for any group of people with an eye for detail and a love of nature and of craftsmanship. To cite just a few, there is Worsley, where the canal system of the country started and where the Packet House and steps bear witness of passenger travel before the days of railways. Prestolee is easily reached, and in this attractive little valley can be seen the now abandoned staircase of locks, the aqueduct and a dozen other canal structures.

East of Manchester there is Fairfield, where the Ashton locks start, and Waterhouses, with the opened-out tunnel, the abandoned locks and aqueduct. South-east is Marple, with its lime kilns and its great flight of locks leading down to the monumental aqueduct. Farther out are Bugsworth and Whaley Bridge, with their ancient plateway and railway links. For those in the centre of Manchester with a few minutes to spare, it is worth tracing the old Manchester and Salford Junction canal from Great Bridgewater Street to its connection with the Irwell beside the fine Victoria and Albert warehouses. It is equally worth walking up the towpath of the Ashton canal, which starts a few hundred yards north of the slope to Piccadilly station.

Whether it is for the history, the architecture, the remoteness even in the town centre, the birds or the wild flowers of the banks, the canals to Manchester offer a rich reward to all who are prepared to seek them out.

2

The Mersey and Irwell Navigation

A group of mountain streams from the Derbyshire Peak District join to form the headwaters of the Mersey, whose tributaries include the Tame, the Goyt and the Etherow. The Irwell drains the highlands of Rossendale in Lancashire, collecting the Croal and the Irk on its way to the junction. The two rivers join some distance west of Manchester and, though the Irwell would appear to carry the greater volume of water, the Mersey retains its name as it swings south-west to Runcorn and from there north-west to Liverpool. Today the rivers flow through miles of industry and are heavily polluted despite recent attempts to clean them. This was not always the case, for salmon used to be caught in Manchester in the eighteenth century. Corbett[7] devotes a chapter to angling and quotes from a lecture his father used to give: 'We heard of a time when fine salmon were caught opposite the New Bailey . . . and we are told of many trout and other fine fish that had been common'.

An old painting of Stickins lock, long since covered by the concrete of Davyhulme, shows the lockhouse amongst trees and green fields in remote countryside. Towns were small and concentrated in the days before the industrial revolution, and villages were separated by rural countryside, much of it not even enclosed. The lower parts of Lancashire and Cheshire were covered by undrained mosses, Chat Moss south of Leigh being a typical example. The need for better communication was therefore great.

The reigns of Charles II and later of George I saw many Bills in

Parliament to improve the navigation of rivers so that coastal vessels could come farther inland. In Lancashire and Cheshire the two minerals which needed a better means of transport were coal and salt. Thus we find that Thomas Steers, who built the first dock in Liverpool, carried out surveys of the Douglas from Wigan, the Weaver from Northwich and the Mersey and Irwell from Manchester. This was in 1712; eight years later an Act was obtained for the Douglas, and in 1721 two further Acts permitted the other rivers to be made navigable.

A river navigation Act was very different from a canal Act, for rivers have always been present and the Act must preserve the rights of landowners, mill owners and others. For instance, the raising of water levels by the building of weirs and locks can flood valuable low-lying pasture, and heavy use of water in locking may take power from water mills. In addition, rivers often form boundaries which must not be changed arbitrarily. Canals, on the other hand, were new to the scene, and there are instances of some being built without an Act of Parliament when they lay entirely within the lands of the canal builder. The canal Act was a kind of compulsory purchase order and it protected rather different rights. Some landowners feared that land drainage might be upset or that streams might dry up, others were concerned about their shooting rights and yet others feared poaching from the canal builders and boatmen.

Though the Mersey and Irwell Navigation Company received their Act in 1721, work did not begin until 1724. Eight weirs were built to raise the water levels over shallows, and short cuts were made round them with locks to lift the boats from one level to the next. Hadfield and Biddle[15] describe how the first boats reached Manchester ten years later and how the company built quays and warehouses just below the town in what is now Water Street in 1740. The Mersey itself was tidal for some distance above Warrington, and the navigation entered the tidal channel at Howley. This was satisfactory when the fortnightly spring tides were flowing, but the intervening neap tides gave too little depth of water for loaded boats to reach the navigation at all.

We are able to catch a glimpse of the early navigation and the boats which used it from the many well known 'Prospects', one of which in the John Rylands library was drawn about 1738. There is considerable artist's licence but it shows Mr Moss's Wharf on the Manchester side of the river some little distance below the bridge and an open barge with a centre mast and a fore-and-aft sail. An earlier example of 1728 comments that the Irwell is soon to be made navigable and shows smaller craft drawn up at this wharf. The boats themselves were sailed with a favourable wind or bowhauled by gangs of men known as halers.

The opening of the Bridgewater canal from Manchester to Runcorn introduced a note of healthy competition, and in 1779 a group of Manchester and Liverpool businessmen bought the river navigation and started a number of improvements. The difficult stretch below Howley lock was cut out by the building of the seven-and-three-quarter-mile Runcorn–Latchford canal, and at Runcorn a basin was built for boats to wait for the tide. This canal was a little above high water spring tide, and boats coming down river had to lock up into it as they do into the Gloucester–Sharpness canal today. This meant that water had to be brought by aqueduct from the Woolston cut to make good all that was lost by locking.

It is in the early nineteenth century that contemporary accounts give us a much clearer impression of the navigation and the boats that used it. Strickland came on a visit from Philadelphia and published his report in 1826.[41] He wrote: 'The Mersey and Irwell Navigation Company's boats (a drawing of one of which accompanies this report) are but twelve feet across the beam and about sixty feet in length. They are built and rigged in such a manner as to exactly fit a lock chamber of thirteen by sixty-five feet. They carry sixty tons, draw but five feet of water, sail very fast, and are capable of contending with the most boisterous of weather. Their masts are made to strike by means of a forestay attached to two double-sheaved blocks, one of which is firmly fixed to the top of the stem. The stay is hove down by a windlass on the forepart of the deck. The boom extends no further out than the after extremity of the rudder, and the stern is made nearly in a vertical line. These vessels are well adapted to the coasting trade and extend their voyages to every part of the island.'

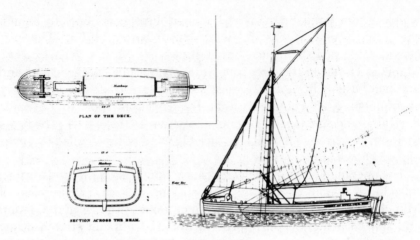

PLAN OF THE DECK.

SECTION ACROSS THE BEAM.

A small Mersey flat of 1826; after Strickland

Manchester Museum has a model of the Weaver flat *Elizabeth* which is clearly very like the boat described here with its vertical-transom stern. It is, however, broader, with a beam of 18 ft 6 in., though the length is still only 65 ft. The rudder extends a further six feet. The wonder is that a boat that is practically flat-bottomed, with very little keel, should have been able to sail round the coast without leeboards. *Elizabeth* was built in 1826 and was used chiefly in the carriage of coal from the St Helens area on the Sankey navigation to Northwich on the Weaver and salt from Northwich down to Liverpool.

We have an interesting sidelight on the navigation in the story of 'Old Billy', the longest-lived canal horse, as told recently by E. L. Seyd.[38] 'Old Billy' was born at Woolston in 1760 and trained to the plough. When two or three years old he appears to have been bought by the Navigation Company and employed to work a gin, an apparatus which, linked with a jib, would form a wharfside crane. He also took his turn in pulling boats, and was kept at work up to the advanced age of fifty-nine, when he was retired to a farm in Latchford. He died in November 1822 at the record age of sixty-two years, and Seyd has produced abundant evidence to show that this age was authentic. 'Old Billy' became famous for his longevity and was painted by two artists of merit, William Bradley and Charles Towne. The Bradley painting shows him with the navigation in the background and an open boat with a mast fairly well forward and a fore-and-aft rig. The Towne painting has a more idealised background, with the river and various sailing craft and undecked barges.

Our next view of the navigation is an account given by Sir George Head[17] in 1836. 'In order to proceed from Liverpool to Manchester by the third and last canal route, I got on board the Eclipse steamer, at the dock of the Mersey and Irwell Navigation, or Old Quay Company, at twenty minutes before nine, and before eleven o'clock we arrived at Runcorn. The basin and docks here, and at Liverpool, belonging to this establishment, by no means equal in appearance those of the Duke of Bridgewater; In fact, a comparison throws them many degrees in the background.

'At Runcorn, indeed, we came to anchor close alongside the packet-boat; an obvious convenience to passengers, compared with the ceremony of consigning their luggage to a porter, and toiling to the top of the hill – the level of the Duke's canal. This advantage, however, is counterbalanced in the long run. The difficulties, in one instance, are all surmounted previous to the commencement of the voyage; in the other, the delay and trouble of passing the numerous locks is experienced during its continuance. This boat is of a heavier construction altogether than that of the Duke, the cabin instead of on the deck, being below, as in ordinary river or sea boats; and it is towed by three horses instead of two; the middle horse moving on between the other two, unridden. Two boys rode . . . without stirrups, resting their feet on the traces, sometimes high, sometimes low, according as the horse lay on his collar. . . . The whole fare from Liverpool to Manchester was . . . 3/6. We left Runcorn precisely at twenty minutes after eleven, and arrived at a quarter before six. . . . Although the course of this navigation chiefly leads through the Mersey and Irwell rivers, the prospect is chiefly shut out by winding, muddy banks, so lofty that at least seventy yards of towrope are used; the extremity of which is fastened high on the mast above the cross-trees. The first artificial cut of the canal commences at starting, and continues for about eight miles; the others on the way are of less extent. Having halted for a short time near the town of Warrington, we continued our passage, with little exception, on the Mersey, till arriving within ten miles of Manchester, at the confluence of the Mersey and Irwell rivers, which two streams are at this point equal in point of width, we proceeded for the rest of the voyage up the latter river.'

At this time the navigation was in excellent condition and was paying regular dividends. The company had reached agreement with its rival, the Bridgewater, to charge similar tolls, and there was plenty of business for both in and around the rapidly growing town of Manchester. Even the coming of George Stephenson's Liverpool and Manchester railway had little effect on the carriage of goods, though the end was in sight for the passenger boats.

In 1844 Lord Francis Egerton bought the navigation on behalf of the Bridgewater company at a price of over half a million pounds, and two years later it was transferred to the Bridgewater company. It was because of this that the Ship Canal Company had to buy both navigations forty years later, as they needed the river course for the construction of their own waterway.

Our last words on the state of the navigation come from Sir Bosdin Leech:[24] 'In view of the advent of railways, every effort was made to improve the navigation and a costly work was carried out in 1840. By widening and deepening, the river was made navigable for vessels of 300 tons burden.' Then, quoting from the *Manchester Guardian* of 1841, 'A vessel arrived in Manchester direct from Dublin with a cargo of potatoes and was discharged at the Old Quay Company's Wharf. . . . The vessel, the Mary, Captain John Hill, having discharged her cargo, will, it is expected, "clear" and sail this day for Dublin with a cargo of coals from . . . Pendleton. Such are probably the small beginnings of Manchester's future greatness as one of the Ports of the United Kingdom.'

Yet, Leech continues, 'In 1882 the river was hopelessly choked with silt and filth. . . . Out of 311 working days, the river was navigable for 50 ton boats for 47 days.' The following year it was not navigable at all throughout the month of October.

We get a very different picture of this charming river for pleasure purposes from the pages of Corbett.[7] There were landing stages at Hunts Bank, below the cathedral, from which small steamers ran pleasure trips to the Pomona Gardens. There were boat-building and boat-hiring firms below Blackfriars Bridge, and boat houses on the Salford side. The whole picture is of a river much used for pleasure right in the centre of the present cities of Manchester and Salford. The New Bailey Landing Stage on the Salford side, opposite the splendid warehouses of Water Street, was said to be the busiest place on the river in the 1850s, for it was from here that the packet boats started for Warrington and Runcorn. Corbett's description of the boats differs slightly from Head's, for he states that they were lightly built, roomy barges about sixty-six feet by fifteen, with two or more horses which went at a brisk trot. They carried goods as well as passengers and would stop almost anywhere to suit their clients.

There were also the Swift Packet Boats, smaller and more lightly built, which were restricted to passengers. Pulled by three horses, they had red-jacketed jockeys, the leader with a horn to clear the way ahead. The horses went at a fast trot and all boats had to drop their towlines and give way to them. Like the cargo-carrying narrow boats, they sometimes erected a large square sail if the wind was right, and the horses had to gallop fast to keep ahead of the boat.

At Regent's Bridge were the boat houses of the important rowing clubs and of the Manchester and Salford Regatta Committee. Contemporary pictures show stands and hundreds of people lining the banks. The Pomona Gardens came next, with their pavilions, restaurants and zoo. Below the gardens, Throstle Nest was the highest lock on the navigation. There was said to be a Roman ford between the gardens and the weir, and this became deeply submerged by the raising of the water level when the lock and weir were built.

Throstle Nest lock was said to be extremely dangerous during floods, for it was built on the Stretford (south) side of the river and the towpath above the weir was on the Salford (north) side. Thus horses had to be unhitched and the boat steered across the river to the lock while the current swept it towards the weir. Corbett himself saw the wrecks of two barges and tells of passengers being taken off at great risk in rowing boats.

Corbett's description of the four miles below Throstle Nest lock is revealing. He states that Trafford Park formed the beautiful south bank of the Irwell, a park with fine trees and wild deer and the hall in full view of the river. These were the days before the Ship Canal had turned it into the largest industrial estate in the world. Furthermore, there were several mansions in wooded gardens on the Salford side before the next lock at Mode Wheel.

The third lock was at Barton, close to Brindley's three-arched stone aqueduct. Stickins lock followed in a six-hundred-yard cut which shortened the river by over a mile. Further locks at Holmes Bridge and Calamanco occurred with fairly short pounds between and, at the latter, the towpath changed sides to the north again and horses had to be taken across by ferry.

Irlam Hall and Fairhills Farm with their orchards and gardens were passed on the old course of the Irwell before its confluence with the Mersey, and Sandywarps cut and lock came next. Two miles farther down was Owlets Nest lock and, below this, Hollins Green Ferry. Close by the ferry was the Boathouse Inn, where rowing men stopped for lunch or tea, frequently taken on the lawns, which reached down to the river. Below Warburton bridge regattas were held annually on a long straight stretch of the river before it was joined by the Bollin. The paired locks of Butchersfield terminated a short channel which cut off a long, almost diamond-shaped loop two miles in length. A further two-mile cut at Woolston shortened the navigation by another two miles of meandering river, and this ended with Paddington lock, which connected once more with the river.

This length of the river was affected by high spring tides above Howley lock and weir, much as the Severn levels can be raised above Gloucester. Corbett describes locking up into the Latchford canal and rowing along the seven miles to the Old Quay at Runcorn.

Today the Irwell navigation has been practically obliterated by the Ship Canal and by the industries, railways and sewage works which have appeared beside it. The Mersey section of the navigation, however, is still remarkably intact. Starting from Manchester, Throstle Nest Lane preserves the name of the site where the highest lock on the navigation was built. It adjoins the roundabout on the

Chester Road and Trafford Road, which runs north to the main docks entrance. The Pomona Gardens are now covered by the Pomona Docks.

Mode Wheel lock lay a few hundred yards north-west of the great locks of that name on the Ship Canal, where now are extensive railway lines. Barton lock lay a little upstream of the original aqueduct, and the lock island appears to form the foundation for the base of the present swing aqueduct. Corbett states in a footnote that the lock cottages of Stickins, Holmes Bridge and Calamanco are still to be seen in the Manchester sewage works, but this was as long ago as 1907. Today they are no more.

The Stickins lock channel cut off two loops of the river, one of which is still visible from the Liverpool Road close to the Barton aerodrome. A little farther to the west, before Irlam is reached, a short stretch of the river can be seen, and a mile south-west of this is a fine stretch of river between Irlam Ferry Road and Fairfield Road. At the eastern end the old Boat Inn is an attractive house and the river is wide and deep. Parkland extends for about a mile, and it is easy to visualise it in Corbett's sculling days. Sandywarps was on the site now occupied by the Irlam steelworks, and the line of the river is clearly visible from the Warburton toll bridge as it crossed the Ship Canal. From here it is much easier to follow the course of the river, which is out in open country.

De Salis[8] gives distances from Rixton junction with the Ship Canal, one and a half miles below Warburton bridge, where the Bollin river comes in from the south. The old navigation here was still used, particularly in Warrington, long after the Ship Canal was open to traffic. From Rixton, the Butchersfield cut is still in water, and the two-mile loop is clearly visible crossing the Ship Canal and extending some distance to the south towards Statham and Lymm. Corbett says in a footnote that the two locks and the lockhouse were entirely destroyed before the end of last century.

The Woolston New Cut is in water from end to end. At the eastern end it is entered from the Mersey by the abandoned Woolston lock, whose stonework is plainly visible. The upper end of the lock opened out on to the curve of the river, but the lock itself is filled in and forms the vegetable garden of the lock cottage. The lower gates are still in place, apparently supporting the garden instead of a lock full of water! There is a good towpath the whole two-mile length of the cut to Paddington lock, which has also been filled in. The stonework here is also clearly visible, and it is possible to measure the lock accurately. It is 17 ft 6 in. wide and 82 ft from gate to gate. Measurements showed that Woolston lock was the same width, and it is reasonable to assume that it was approximately the same length.

The Old Quay, Runcorn, Mersey and Irwell Navigation, about 1895

The towpath returned to the south side of the canal at Paddington lock and immediately crossed the Mersey on top of the wooden trough that formed the aqueduct for the feeder for the Latchford canal. This feeder, with its small bridges, runs along the south side of the river, a few feet above it, and is still carrying water. Its final connection with the Latchford canal is piped.

Half a mile down the river the deep, clear water of the Latchford canal joins the south bank of the Mersey, and Manor lock is complete and looks as if it might still be worked. It is 19 ft wide and 84 ft from gate to gate. The gates, each of which has two paddles worked from a small bridging platform on the upper side of the gate, meet at a fairly acute angle. Thus, allowing room for the sill and for the gates to swing open, it would seem that the maximum size of barge would be 75 ft to 80 ft long by 18 ft 6 in. beam. The narrower locks on the Woolston cut would take a barge of approximately the same length with a beam of 17 ft. Yet De Salis gives the maximum size of boats as 72 ft 8 in. by 16 ft 4 in. from Rixton junction to Warrington, and a similar length but two feet wider through Latchford. On both, the draught is given as 5 ft 6 in. In neither case would a boat of 300 tons have been able to use the navigation.

The Latchford canal runs south-west to the Ship Canal and joins it at Twenty Steps lock, which measures 85 ft by 19 ft. Constructed by the Ship Canal when it was built, it was the entrance to what was left of the old navigation and was useful in serving the wharfs of Warrington. The rest of the Latchford canal was then of little value as a navigation and was abandoned. It can be followed westwards, reedy but still mostly in water, through the long island between the Ship Canal and the Mersey estuary. About three miles east of Runcorn its channel was taken by the Ship Canal, except for a small loop with a lone black corrugated iron warehouse near the Old Quay swing bridge.

As mentioned earlier, the lowest lock on the navigation before the Latchford canal was built was at Howley, and this lock is still fairly

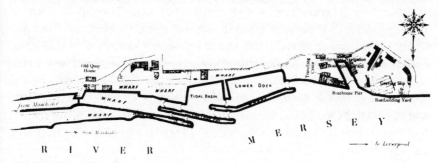

Old Quay docks, Runcorn, 1878

complete. The towpath along the Mersey below Manor lock continues on the south side of the river, which bends sharply to the south after half a mile. An extensive wharf and fine warehouses with huge canopies are on the north side at the corner. Two hundred yards beyond the bend the towpath crosses the river on a lightly built suspension bridge and then continues a further three hundred yards to the Howley cut. Immediately beyond the cut is Howley weir, which is a most impressive fall at low water. Howley cut is very short, little over one hundred yards long, and is positioned at right-angles to the river, immediately above the weir. We can picture the turn into the cut as a hazardous exercise in time of flood, though the weir is overtopped by the spring tides at high water.

Howley lock is at the western end of the cut and is almost the same size as Manor lock. Beautifully constructed, the masonry sides are still in excellent condition, but the lock itself is used only for drainage. The two top gates are chained back and a large sluice crosses the whole width of the lock above the sill. The north side bottom gate is open and that on the south is missing. At low tide the lock appears very deep indeed and the water below a mere trickle.

Most of the area between the river and Latchford canal is occupied by Victoria Park, and the towpaths of both navigations make attractive walks. With the waters held up by the weir, the river is wide and deep, and it is surprising that Warrington has not made more use of the area. The north frontage, dominated by the spire of the church and the fine warehouses, could be very beautiful, and the three-arched bridge above Manor lock is a graceful structure. The whole scene is Thames-scale. There was a small sailing craft tacking up the river when I paid my first visit, but the town seems unaware of this gem. Perhaps when pollution is reduced, and salmon find their way back, Warrington may once more be proud of the river heritage. Below Howley the river is completely tidal and winds its way to the estuary and the Irish Sea.

3

The Bridgewater Canal

There is much controversy as to which is the first canal in England, some claiming the Fossdyke in Lincolnshire, some the Exeter canal, some the Sankey navigation from St Helens, and some the Bridgewater. Suffice it to say that the Roman Fossdyke was built as a drainage channel and used for navigation, like so many similar dykes in Holland. The Exeter canal was a river navigation, a cut a few miles in length with locks to avoid the difficult tidal stretches, and the Sankey navigation, though a true canal, was built alongside a river under a river navigation Act. The Bridgewater was the first English canal to be built under the powers of a canal Act and was intended to be truly independent of rivers, except for those used to feed it.

As mentioned in the introduction, road communications in the Manchester area were bad, especially in the rainy seasons, and the town needed coal dug from pits only a few miles away. Coal is a heavy and bulky commodity, and the possibilities of water carriage were obvious for the pits situated near the Mersey and Irwell Navigation. Such pits occurred round Worsley and Walkden, and an Act of Parliament was obtained in 1737 to make the Worsley Brook navigable from the Irwell. This would have allowed coal from the first Duke of Bridgewater's mines to be carried into Manchester and Salford. The brook itself was some distance from the pits, and a railway or plateway with horse-drawn tubs would have been necessary to carry the coal to the navigation. In any case, the navigation was never made.

Seventeen years later a group of Manchester businessmen tried to get powers to build a canal from Wigan through Leigh to Salford, but opposition from landowners was great. Hadfield and Biddle[15] make the point that taking water from the Irwell above Manchester was crucial in the decision against the building of this canal. The year before, an Act had been passed to improve the roads in the coal-mining areas, but years were to elapse before road surfaces were such as to permit the transport of heavy loads at all times of the year, and there was still only the power of horses to draw the vehicles.

One great landowner who was enthusiastic about the building of canals was the young third Duke of Bridgewater. Much has been written of his background, his delicate youth, his early unsuccessful love affairs, his Grand Tour, on which he saw the Canal du Midi, and his retreat from London to the Worsley estates. Hugh Malet[26] tells this interesting story fully, and others have referred to it. Suffice it to say that the duke's interest in his mines and in the development of canals for the carriage of heavy goods revolutionised transport throughout the country. He was fortunate in his Worsley agent, John Gilbert, and later in the appointment of James Brindley, the millwright and self-taught engineer who surmounted the many problems for him. There is controversy to this day as to which of the two men was the more deeply concerned in the actual building of the canal. There is little doubt, however, that the driving force was the duke himself, who used every penny of his fortune and borrowed heavily to complete the work.

In 1759, when the duke was only twenty-three years of age, the first Bridgewater Act was obtained for a two-pronged canal to run on the one hand from Worsley to Salford and, on the other, south-west to the Irwell. The preamble to the Act reads as follows: 'An Act to enable the Most Noble Francis, Duke of Bridgewater, to make a navigable Cut or Canal from a certain place in the Township of Salford to or near Worsley Mill and Middlewood in the Manor of Worsley and to or near a place called Holmes Ferry in the County Palatine of Lancaster'. It contrasts markedly with the 1737 Act: 'An Act for making navigable the River or Brook called Worsley Brook, in the Township of Worsley in the County Palatine of Lancaster, to the

River Irwell in the said County'. In the 1759 Act the duke was to make the canal at his own expense and was to take no water from the Irwell. Coal was to be brought from Worsley to sell at not more than 4*d* a hundredweight to the inhabitants of Manchester and Salford.

The duke bought land in Salford for quays, the work started immediately and a few months later James Brindley was brought in. Whether or not it is a coincidence, before the end of the year the duke had had second thoughts on his line, and 1760 saw a second Act to carry the canal across the Irwell and bring it to the edge of Manchester. Such a crossing had not been attempted in England before, and many people were sceptical as to its achievement. Brindley had no doubts, however, and is said to have demonstrated to the parliamentary select committee with a model made from cheese. He would keep the water from leaking through the arches by lining the channel with puddled clay, a material which proved so satisfactory that it is still used at the present time. The aqueduct was opened in July 1761.

The bicentenary brochure produced by the Bridgewater Department of the Manchester Ship Canal Company in 1961 quotes from the *Manchester Mercury* as follows: 'On Friday last His Grace the Duke of Bridgewater, with the Earl of Stamford and several other gentlemen, came to Barton to see the water turned into the Canal over the River Irwell, which drew together a large number of spectators, and it is with pleasure that we can inform the public that the experience answered the most sanguine expectations of everyone present. As soon as the water had risen to the level of the Canal a large boat carrying upwards of fifty tons was towed along the new part of the Canal over arches across the River Irwell which were so firm, secure and compact that not a single drop of water could be perceived to ouze thro' any part of them, although the surface of the Canal is thirty eight feet above the navigable river under it. This canal will be carried to Manchester with all expedition and we are creditably informed will be completed before Lady-Day next, every seeming difficulty now being removed, and that in the meantime the subterraneous Navigation to the Collieries will be perfected so that we may expect to have a supply of coals as will reduce considerably the price of coal to the consumer and this work will be of very great use as well as ornament to the town of Manchester.'

In 1763, in a letter to the same paper, 'C.S.' wrote: 'I have lately been viewing the artificial wonders of London, but none gave me so much pleasure as the Duke of Bridgewater's Navigation. His projector, the ingenious Mr. Brindley, has indeed made such improvements in this way, as are truly astonishing. At Barton bridge, he has erected a navigable canal in the air; for it is as high as the tops of the trees. Whilst I was surveying it with a mixture of wonder and delight, four barges passed me in the space of about three minutes, two of them being chained together, and dragged by two horses, who went on the terras of the canal, whereon, I must own, I durst hardly venture to walk, as I almost trembled to behold the River Irwell beneath me.'

There are a number of drawings showing boats passing along the

The original Barton aqueduct over the Irwell navigation, about 1890

one navigation on the aqueduct over the other. One of the more onerous clauses in the Act prohibited the builders from obstructing the lower navigation while carrying out the construction of the aqueduct. To balance this, the Irwell was not expected to shoot down floods at inconvenient moments.

The canal was open to Longford Bridge, Stretford, in 1761 and to Manchester two years later. Extensive wharfs and warehouses were built at Castlefield, at the western end of Deansgate, and one such warehouse was demolished as recently as 1960.

The short branch built south-westwards to Longford Bridge enabled coal to be carried by road into Manchester until the length to Castlefield was completed, and also into Cheshire. The real point of this, and perhaps of the Irwell crossing, became clear in 1762, when another Act was obtained, this time to extend the canal westwards across the Mersey and Bollin rivers and to drop down a flight of locks to reach the tidal river at a place called Hempstones, a short distance upstream from Runcorn. Here, then, was competition with the Mersey and Irwell navigation, providing an alternative water route from Manchester to Liverpool, a route where levels could be controlled, where floods would not occur and where drought should have little effect. The whole canal was to be on one level at approximately eighty seven feet above mean sea level until it finally descended by a series of ten locks to the estuary. One more change was to take place before the building of the locks was put in hand. Brindley had surveyed a line across the country to connect the Mersey with the Trent, and an Act was obtained in 1766 to build this canal. A clause was inserted to link it with the Bridgewater at Preston Brook, the duke varying his own line and building his locks at Runcorn instead of Hempstones. By this means he had some control over the Trent and Mersey canal and took his toll on goods passing on to his navigation. The Trent and Mersey gained his support for their Bill in Parliament (there was a rival scheme) and saved a considerable sum of money in the building of locks. The locks themselves were open in 1774 and the whole canal in 1776.

We can get a very clear picture of the Bridgewater canal throughout its long history from a variety of sources. Around 1773 Josiah

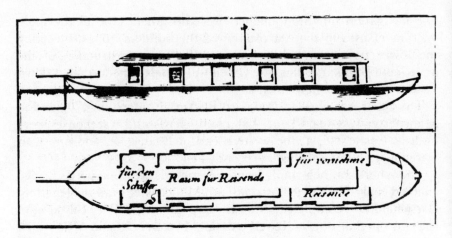

A packet or passenger boat of the Bridgewater canal before 1780; after Hogrewe. Note the cabins for the two classes and for the captain

Wedgwood carried out an inspection of the Trent and Mersey canal, still unfinished. His diary (Meteyard[29]) notes: 'We are to visit Runcorn and from thence to proceed on His Grace's boat to Worsley. . . .' 'From Warrington to Manchester, the Duke has set up two passage boats, one carries passengers at a shilling each. The other is divided into three rooms and the rates are 2/6 per head for the best room, 10*d* and 12*d* and it is the pleasantest and cheapest mode you can conceive. We next visited Worsley which has the appearance of a considerable seaport town.'

In 1780 Johann Ludevig Hogrewe came to England to examine the canal system and published his results in Hanover.[18] His description of the Bridgewater canal particularly around Runcorn is enhanced by his beautiful engravings. In particular, plate 7 illustrates the Runcorn locks and weirs, the emergency gates and even one of the passenger boats. His dimensions and scale are not accurate, and he may have confused the sizes of both locks and boats with those of the rival navigation. He described the locks as occurring in pairs, each lock 96 ft by 16 ft with a rise of 8 ft and each pair separated by a basin to allow the boats to pass. The walls were of brick, based on and capped with stone, and the closed gates were at right-angles to one another.

Ground paddles brought water into the higher of each pair of locks and from these to the lower locks, but gate paddles in the bottom gates of the lower locks were used to empty them. The sluices in the gates were attached to vertical ratchets, and those controlling the ground paddles were raised with a worm gear similar to a number still to be found on the Leeds and Liverpool canal. As exceptionally high tides rose above the water level in a full bottom lock, there were chains on the beams to keep them closed. Circular weirs like those still used on the Staffs. and Worcester canal were placed strategically to carry off excess water.

The barges using the canal were said to be 70–80 ft long and 14–15 ft wide and to carry sixty to eighty tons. They were said to be partly decked and to be towed by two horses or to sail as far as Liverpool and even up the coast. Clearly, here, Hogrewe was describing Mersey flats, the larger of which were not able to use the canal. In greater detail he described the passenger boats, which were covered barges similar to those used in Holland, 56 ft long by 8 ft beam, with a height above water of 7 ft. They were pulled by one horse at about five miles an hour and covered the journey to Manchester in eight hours despite two stops to change horses. The rate at that time was 3s 6d for the fore cabin and 2s 3d for the second cabin; the 'skipper' had his own rear cabin. Passengers in the fore cabin could also sit in the bows in the open air. There was a towing mast amidships which could also be used to carry a sail, and an ingenious arrangement of a pulley at its base with a rope from the sail to the stern allowing the skipper to hoist or lower the sail without leaving the tiller.

The floodgates were also described and illustrated. These were gates set in specially constructed narrows and lying normally on the bed of the canal. They were placed at the ends of aqueducts and embankments, and, if a burst occurred, the rush of water through the narrows lifted them up and closed them tightly against an iron-shod recess.

One hundred years later, Corbett[7] published a photograph of the Earl of Ellesmere's pleasure boat, which was specially built for the Queen's visit in 1851. Hadfield and Biddle[15] describe the boat, which was 45 ft in length, with a long central saloon and a canopy over the forward cockpit. Both bow and stern were ornamental, and she was drawn by a pair of grey horses. The boat was kept in the boathouse at Worsley, but although the boathouse has been preserved the boat itself is no more. it was used for a time as the directors' inspection boat, and later with a petrol engine to take parties of people round the Manchester docks.

Another vessel of great interest which suffered much the same fate as recently as 1960 was the famous packet boat *Duchess-Countess*. Fortunately Mr John Scholes of the Transport Museum at Clapham had her measured while she was lying on the banks of the Shropshire Union canal being used as a hen house! Manchester Museum had an accurate model built by Mr D. Sattin to a scale of one-sixteenth full size. This is now in the Boat Museum at Ellesmere Port.

Our next glimpse of the Bridgewater canal is through the eyes of Sir George Head,[17] who was extremely interested in the canal system. He made a number of journeys on packet boats at a time when the

The Earl of Ellesmere's barge at Worsley

railways were already beginning to take their custom. The Liverpool and Manchester railway was already in being and could make the journey much more quickly, though with less comfort. Head started from Liverpool, taking the steamer to Runcorn, and was delighted at the appearance of the two flights of locks, with craft seen one above the other mounting towards the summit. Here the packet boat was waiting for the passengers, who had walked up the lock side. It was clean and tidy, with first and second class cabins and a flat roof with benches for those who liked to ride on top. He wrote that 'the boat was towed at a rate of about five miles an hour by a couple of clumsy cart horses, driven beyond their natural pace'! Two small boys acted as jockeys and kept jumping on and off the horses for the whole six hours of the voyage. The canal itself was said to be 'black as the Styx and absolutely pestiferous' for the last dozen miles into Manchester, owing to pollution, much of it from the Medlock.

From the early days of the production of coal gas at the beginning of

The Earl of Ellesmere's barge in the boathouse at Worsley; before 1906

the nineteenth century the by-products – tar and ammonia – were simply poured into the nearest stream. Later it was found that the tar could be used and sold as a bituminous paint and pollution eased a little, but many years were to elapse before the nuisance was eradicated completely.

Head then took the packet boat from Manchester to Liverpool through Worsley, Leigh and Wigan, a journey starting at six in the morning and taking fourteen hours. The boats were just the same as those on the Runcorn route, and breakfast and dinner were provided on board at a shilling for each meal. At Wigan the boat stayed to load for half an hour, and the town was judged 'a compound of villainous smells', the journey being dull and tedious. At Scarisbrick bridge, near Ormskirk, omnibuses and luggage carts waited for the boat's arrival to take people to the seaside at Southport, about six miles to the west. The canal terminated in a basin close to the Liverpool canal wharfs, and at that time there was no connection with the docks. This was to come a few years later when the Stanley locks were built and the canal was linked with the sea.

About twenty years later Corbett[7] described how scullers from the Mersey and Irwell navigation would lift out their boats at the Old Quay Company's Runcorn docks and carry them up the steep streets on to the Bridgewater canal higher up the hillside. They would stay Saturday night in 'the cosy rooms of Wilsons Hotel', have a quiet

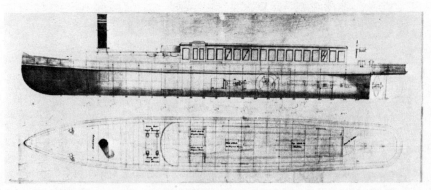

A Bridgewater Canal steam tug, 1893

game of bowls on the lawn and enjoy an excellent dinner, followed by a 'smoke and song and liquid refreshment'. Next morning they would attend an open-air service 'much frequented by sailors and canal boatmen'. In the early days they would even enjoy a swim in the canal, but pollution was later to put a stop to this.

The row back along the canal to Manchester meant keeping an eye open for packet boats and flyboats, with their trotting horses, and later the little steam tugs with their trains of barges. In 1882 pleasure boating was prohibited on the canal, as it was so easy for damage to be caused by the towed barges swinging on the curves. In Castlefield the old packet station was described as like a small railway station, with its waiting rooms and parcel and luggage offices. Though the passenger services had finished many years before the turn of the century, several flyboats still carried fruit and vegetables from farms and orchards on the canal side until the 1920s, the *Duchess-Countess* among them. The flyboats had priority over the slower barges, but gave way to the packet boats.

A Bridgewater barge captain's cabin, 1887; after Tomlinson

Another description of the barges and their people was given by Walter Tomlinson[44] in 1887 when he made a trip in the barge *Jemima Ann* from Manchester to Stockton Heath, near Warrington. The boat was horse-drawn, with a captain, mate and a couple of boys, and was shafted out of 'Knott Mill Basin' (Castlefield). The smells were not very salubrious until the boat reached the open country, but then the journey became a pleasant one. Occasionally a steam tug was met, pulling three barges, each with two men aboard. The captain's cabin in the stern was described in some detail, and a sketch of it was published, showing the near-vertical ladder, the fixed seats on three sides and the stove on the fourth. The seats themselves were lockers, there were numerous cupboards, and the door of the crockery cupboard was hinged to form a drop-down table. There was a sliding panel on one side which uncovered a recess for the bed, six feet by two. The walls were panelled, painted and grained. The mate's cabin in the bows was smaller.

Tomlinson was interested in the lives and conditions of the boat people, and found that some were paid by the trip and some a weekly wage with a commission. A captain in full employment might earn from 32*s* to £2 a week and his mate two-thirds of that sum. The trips were mostly local, for the barges seldom left the Bridgewater canal. Despite this, some captains took their wives to work with them instead of hiring a mate, a custom that had been adopted by narrowboatmen many years earlier. There was a fair amount of traffic, and conditions were considered to be reasonably good, though the chief complaint was that the captain spent so much of his time away from home. Many of the captains were temperate men and the majority could read and write. Doubtless this was also due to the fact that so many were shore-based and, unlike the narrowboatmen, seldom far from home.

Starting today from the extensive basins in Castlefield, the dockside is very different from its appearance in the days of Head and Tomlinson. There is little commercial traffic – even the name of Abbott, carriers for generations, is no longer seen in Potato Wharf – most of the little arms are silted up and abandoned, and the great warehouses have gone. There is still plenty of activity, however, for it remains the base for the Bridgewater Department of the Ship Canal Company. A short distance westwards is the Hulme lock, which links the canal with the Irwell and the Manchester docks. Until the early 1960s there were three locks, each with a fall of 4 ft, but at that time the grain traffic from the docks to Kellogg's factory in Trafford Park was so heavy that they were replaced by a single lock 12 ft fall beneath the railway arches. Today this traffic has taken to the roads. The river Medlock, carrying excess water from the canal, enters the Irwell at this point.

The canal is dominated by the railway, which stands above and beside it on the South Junction viaduct, and by large buildings on its south side. After half a mile the railway crosses over and the canal runs between grassed paths close to the Pomona docks. Factories, works, railway sidings and the famous Manchester United football ground are passed, though the game is hidden from view by the tall stands! The canal then divides, the right branch leading to Worsley and the left to Runcorn. The junction has the romantic name of 'Water's Meeting', though the actual place is less romantic, with its railway bridges, its industry, its weed and floating rubbish.

Taking the left-hand route, the canal passes beneath Longford bridge, once to have been the Cheshire terminus, and swings right past Rathbone's repair yard with its covered dry dock where fleets of wooden barges have had their major overhauls. A mile beyond, the canal crosses the Mersey valley on a long, straight embankment and aqueduct and is itself crossed by the M63 motorway. The Watch House Cruising Club occupies a pleasant little canal building on the north-east side. Then, after two gentle turns, it enters the three-mile straight which extends almost to the centre of Altrincham.

Even though this part of Cheshire has some large centres of population, most of the rest of the canal runs through attractive countryside. Swinging round Dunham Park on a sturdy embankment, it crosses the river Bollin on one of many small aqueducts. This was the scene of the disastrous breach in 1971, when the south side of the embankment adjoining the Bollin aqueduct gave way. The rushing torrent from both sides eroded deep channels in the centre of the embankment, and sand, gravel and rocks were washed out over the field below. The company put in stop planks at the bridge narrows as soon as possible, but a great deal of damage had been done, and several boats were left dry on the bottom. These stop planks are wooden shutters long enough to slide into grooves in the stone sides of the canal and cranes are sited to lift them into position.

For some time there was uncertainty as to whether the breach would be repaired, and the Inland Waterways Association organised a meeting on the site and a rally of boats at Lymm the following year to focus attention on the importance of the whole canal. All turned out well, and the Manchester Ship Canal Company built an excellent concrete channel 20 ft wide for about three hundred yards and reopened it in 1973.

The Lymm Cruising Club have a long line of moorings at Agden Bridge, and further moorings and a fine new clubhouse at Lymm itself. The village is charming, with attractive houses, and is linked

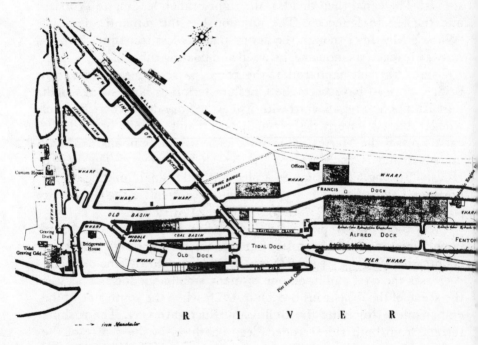

Bridgewater docks, Runcorn, 1878

with Altrincham by a good bus service. To the geologist it is important for the outcrop of certain sandstones on whose surfaces have been found the footprints of creatures extinct now for about one hundred and sixty million years! The canal then passes beneath the M6 motorway and the banks are well wooded. Though less than one hundred feet above sea level, it gives the impression of being on much higher ground, for there are long views across the Mersey valley.

Beyond Stockton Heath and the deep wooded cutting of Walton is the atomic energy establishment at Daresbury, a good example of a modern works built attractively in rural surroundings. It needed to be near a source of water for cooling purposes, and the canal fitted the requirements exactly. The canteen has been built on a bluff looking north over the canal and Mersey, and the lawns sweep down the slope to a promenade on the water's edge. The village of Daresbury lies behind, and here Lewis Carroll's father was once vicar. He is said to

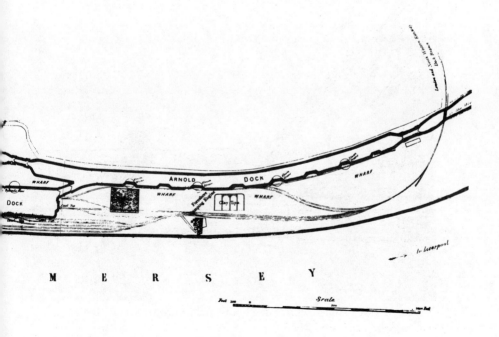

The old bridge, Monton, near Eccles

Worsley Packet House, with mine boats moored near, about 1890

have been interested in the boat people and he organised special services for them, using a barge as a floating chapel.

The canal divides at Preston Brook, linking with the Trent and Mersey on the south and with Runcorn on the north-west. There are some interesting basins and warehouses beyond the M6 motorway and a large, well laid out marina. The canal terminates at Runcorn, for the locks are now closed. One of the last pleasure boatmen to use them was John Seymour, who described a rather perilous journey in his *Voyage into England*.[39] Unfortunately the earlier set of locks had been abandoned some years before: they had lain outside the development area and could have been retained if they had still been usable.

Had we forked to the right at Waters Meeting we should have cruised through the great industrial estate of Trafford Park and crossed the Irwell on the Barton swing aqueduct (described on p. 120). From there we should have passed through Patricroft, where

Worsley Packet House and steps today

Queen Victoria went aboard Lord Ellesmere's barge on her visit to Eccles and Worsley.

Worsley, today, is still a charming village even though the motorway strides over so much of it. The Green with its attractive houses is little changed, the ancient half-timbered Court House stands on the corner, the Packet House commands the curve in the canal as it did when the passenger boats reached it from Manchester and Wigan, and the stone steps to the boats have been cleaned and restored. Lord Ellesmere's boathouse still stands, and a short walk past the Packet house leads to Worsley Delph, where the two tunnels can still be seen in the vertical rock face. This too has been cleared and cleaned up, though the ancient boats no longer lie there at rest.

The remaining five miles past Boothstown and Astley Green to Leigh are something of an anticlimax. The mining of coal has caused pronounced subsidence, and the canal banks have had to be built up high above the surrounding countryside. At Boothstown there was once a much smaller underground canal system, and coal from Astley Green was carried by barge and narrow boat until quite recently. At the wharf were a number of very primitive narrow boats whose construction was developed from that of the starvationer. These, too, carried their coal in boxes which could be lifted in and out of the boat by crane and, like those on the Manchester, Bolton and Bury canal, were early examples of containerisation.

The cotton and coal town of Leigh marks the junction of the Bridgewater canal with an arm of the Leeds and Liverpool, which continues on to Wigan and to the two great cities which gave it its name. So a canal which started as a means of carrying Worsley coal to Salford and then Manchester is now an essential link between the navigations of the Midlands and those of the north of England.

4

The Underground Canals of Worsley

Perhaps as famous in its day as the Duke of Bridgewater's canal from Worsley to Manchester and Runcorn was the series of underground canals tapping his coal seams at Walkden. Where the former was constructed to carry his coals to the markets, the latter were concerned with their actual extraction from beneath the ground. Hugh Malet[26] and Frank Mullineux[32] have both described the background to the scheme. The mines themselves had been exploited from at least the seventeenth century, and Malet emphasises the problems of keeping them sufficiently dry for men to work. One method was to bucket the water out as it collected from underground springs, and another was to drive a small drainage tunnel into the hillside from a lower level and allow the water to run out of its own accord. The mines of Walkden, adjacent to the lower ground of the Mersey valley, were ideally suited to such a method, and a tunnel, or sough, had already been made by the first Duke of Bridgewater's agent.

Mullineux considers that as soon as work started on the Bridgewater canal the idea probably occurred to the third Duke and his agent, John Gilbert, to enlarge an existing sough or to drive a new one of such size that it could combine the functions of carriage of coal with those of drainage. We know that the work on the first underground canal started at approximately the same time as the Bridgewater itself and was continued until some time after 1842. Malet states that a journey in the dark attracted many visitors, including the nobility and even the king of Denmark. We are fortunate that some of these visitors left detailed accounts of what they saw.

One of the first was Gabriel Jars,[22] who came to Worsley in 1765. Having given the location of the mines and the dip and strike of the coal seams (they run from morn to eve and dip towards mid-day!), he notes that a tunnel had been driven into the hillside to carry off water and to exploit the seams. This had already crossed three seams, one of which was workable a mile from the entrance. The tunnel was still being driven forward with the intention of exploiting other seams, one of which was known to be seven feet thick. The tunnel was lined with brick and lime mortar throughout, and debouched into a navigable canal which already extended ten miles to Manchester. If necessary it was possible to let the water out of the tunnel by raising a sluice, and specially designed long, narrow boats were constructed to work in the tunnel and on the coal face. A good sandstone quarry formed the entrance, and limestone occurred near by, suitable for making cement.

This is the first account to mention the special boats which came to be known later as 'starvationers', some say because they were narrow and their ribs showed. The mention of the sluice is also interesting, though it seems unlikely that the tunnel could be emptied in this way. We know from later accounts that sluices were used to build up a head of water which could carry the boats out into the delph as each sluice was raised.

As time went on, a second tunnel was driven at a higher level parallel to and almost immediately above the main tunnel, though this never extended as far as the surface. The two were to be linked by an inclined plane which quickly became one of the great engineering wonders of the world. In 1800 Sir Francis Henry Egerton,[11] nephew of the Duke of Bridgewater, read a paper before the Royal Society of Arts describing the plane in detail. This was of such interest that it was also published in France in 1803, and it gave a clear picture of this interesting structure while it was working. A summary of his paper is as follows.

The underground canals of Worsley and Walkden were then on two levels, the main level extending some twelve miles, including the side extensions into the coal seams and the upper, some thirty-five and a half yards higher, for approximately six miles. The two were linked by an inclined plane so that boats from the upper level could reach the main level, and from this the surface at Worsley Delph, without disturbing their loads of coal. Before the plane was built, boxes of coal from the boats in the upper level had to be winched by hand down a shaft to waiting boats on the main canal beneath.

A site for the plane was chosen on a thick bed of grit dipping down at an angle of one in four. Upon this some 453 ft of rails were laid with double tracks for the upper 282 ft, the tracks separated by a brick wall with regular openings, built right up to the roof. On the lower part of the plane the track was single before it ran into the main canal. The total width of the plane was 19 ft where the track was double and 10 ft only where it was single. The height above the rails was 8 ft. The rails were metal-covered and flanged and rested on sleepers fixed into the rock floor.

At the top of the incline were two locks with sloping floors, each 54 ft long and just under 9 ft wide, separated by a 3 ft thick wall which was built up to 9 in. above water level. The locks had sloping floors, so that the water was $4\frac{1}{2}$ ft deep at the top and 8 ft deep adjoining the plane. The roof above the locks was 21 ft high to accommodate the machinery. Above the locks, a great drum 4 ft 11 in. in diameter was set horizontally, and around this passed a hawser $2\frac{1}{2}$ in. thick. Hooks at each end of the hawser were for attachment to the boats on their carriages.

A large-diameter brake wheel was attached centrally to the drum and geared to a very much smaller pinion fixed to the wall. The gearing was such that only a small effort was needed to start the boats moving and to control their speed on the incline. At the bottom of the incline the rails ran down into the water to a depth of 6 ft 9 in. to allow the boats to float from their carriages.

The carriages were 30 ft long and 7 ft 4 in. wide, with four solid cast-iron wheels which rested on the rails. The boats carried up to twelve tons of coal and, as the boat itself weighed four tons and the carriage five, the total weight on the rails was twenty-one tons. The actual time for each boat to be transported from the upper to the lower canal was sixteen minutes, and as many as thirty boats could be moved in this way in an eight-hour shift. Three types of boats were used in the workings, carrying seven, eight and a half and twelve tons respectively.

The construction of the plane was started in September 1795 and completed ready for use in October 1797.

This account is of interest in giving details of the construction and working of the plane, though there is less information on the working of the locks and we have to wait for later accounts for a more complete description. It is also the first mention that three sizes of boats were in use.

A few years later, J. M. Dutens[10] visited Worsley. At this period there were still two levels only, the lower or main level, now extended to fifteen miles, and the upper, still only six miles. They were described as 10 ft 6 in. wide and 8 ft 8 in. high, lined with bricks for nine-tenths of their length.

He described the plane very fully, comparing and contrasting it with those of Ketley and The Hay in Shropshire, pointing out the fact that it would have been very difficult and expensive to have operated an underground lift, particularly in a coal mine, with a steam engine. His illustration (plate 5) was more detailed than Egerton's. His actual descriptions of the plane, the locks, the rails, the carriages and the boats tally closely with Egerton's and were probably lifted straight out of the published paper. The final point of interest is a statement that the whole machine was operated by two men only, one in charge of the actual mechanism who also opened the lock gates, and the other who worked the various sluices for filling and emptying the locks. Water for the locks came from natural drainage and from three reservoirs constructed for the purpose.

The most complete account of the canals, the mines and the boats together with the methods of construction and of mining the coal was written by two French mining engineers, Henri Fournel and Isidore Dyévre, in 1842.[13] They came to Worsley in February of that year to make a thorough study of the whole system. Henri Fournel was already a distinguished mining engineer in his early forties who was to become Inspector General of the Corps Royale des Mines. He was

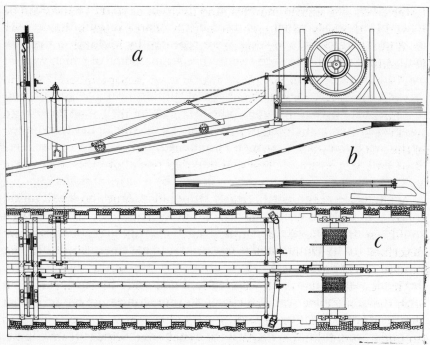

The underground inclined plane. (*a*) The upper part of the diagram shows
the top lock in section. The lock itself has a sloping floor and the boat rests
upon the trolley. On the left is the guillotine gate beneath which it will pass
and the ground paddle to let out the water. On the right is the mitred top
gate, the drum with its cable and the great toothed wheel with its brake. (*b*)
Centre right is a small-scale section and plan of the entire plane. (*c*) The two
locks in plan, with their rails, their guillotine bottom gates and mitred top
gates, their paddle gear and the great drum. The drawing, by Mrs D. Hirst,
is taken from Dutens's plate 5

widely travelled, having visited and published work on mining in both
Algeria and Texas, and there is little doubt that his Worsley visit was
significant. We know less about Dyévre except that he too was a
mining engineer and would appear to have been the junior partner.
Their memoir suggests that the purpose of the visit was a thorough
inspection to see how such methods might be applied to coal mining
in France.

They first described the position of the mines and noted the dip and strike of the rocks, which included fifteen seams varying between 21 in. and 7 ft thick. These rocks were repeated by faulting so that the main canal actually crossed twenty-five seams, some of which were of poor quality.

The canals were then both the oldest subterranean navigations and the most extensive in Europe. When they made their visit there were three levels, the main level from Worsley Delph, the upper level linked by the inclined plane, by then abandoned, and a third, lower level described as a series of canalised galleries one above the other. This lowest level was linked with the main level by a series of shafts.

The main level ran north, nearly straight for three and a half miles, with passing places every quarter of a mile. The tunnel was 8 ft high and 9 ft wide, with water 3 ft 7 in. deep. This width is rather less than that recorded by Dutens and is more likely to have been accurate. The summit of the arch was 4 ft 5 in. above the level of the water. Where the rock was gritstone it was left unlined and the roof was often higher, but in other places the roof and sometimes the entire tunnel was lined with one or two layers of brick.

Sluices were placed at intervals to hold back the water and to divide the canal into a series of pounds. These brought about slight differences of level and could be used to produce a current. A side gallery was cut into the rock by each sluice, which the boatmen could then raise or lower. The total mileage of the main canal together with the side branches running east and west along the strike was given as eighteen miles.

The upper level ran a little farther north than the main level (the seams were dipping south) and totalled ten miles in length together with its east and west branches. The authors commented that the inclined plane linking the two, though abandoned and a total ruin, was so celebrated that they were 'struck dumb'!

The two engineers were fortunate in seeing a third and lowest level actually under construction. It was 200 ft below the main level and, with its side canals, already extended between ten and twelve miles. The tunnels themselves were smaller in section and the water only 2 ft 10 in. deep. In the construction of the tunnel the arch was only a single brick thick, and the dimensions were 7 ft high and 6 ft 6 in. wide. They reached this level from Tonge's Field pit and recorded a large chamber near the pit bottom built as a dock for boats which had had to be lowered down the shaft, as there was no connecting plane and no level link with the outside world.

The next section of the memoir described the methods of mining the coal and bringing it to the nearest canal to be floated away. Two galleries were driven up the dip of the seam perhaps ninety yards apart and a third was then driven equidistant from the two. About forty feet up the slope, cross-galleries were driven parallel with the canal, and a further forty feet up a second set of cross-galleries were driven, leaving the seam in huge rectangular blocks. The miners would then start in the uppermost cross-galleries and take out the coal, working down the dip slope. A block of coal twenty to forty feet wide would be left adjoining the canal to ensure that no damage or subsidence occurred at this point. The rest of the roof would be supported by pit props but would eventually subside.

The coal was hewn in large lumps and separated from the smaller pieces, which were riddled in circular sieves. It was then loaded by children into large rectangular baskets, each on an iron sled runner and dragged down the dip slope and along the galleries to the canal. Here were waiting tub boats (*bateaux à bennes*), each boat having six wooden tubs approximately three feet square and twenty-two inches deep with a capacity of about six hundredweight. The baskets were carefully emptied into the tubs and the boat moved to a pit shaft where a crane could lift each tub to the main level to be placed on larger boats each carrying up to thirty-three tubs.

The engineers then described the boats, which were of three sizes. The smallest were the little tub boats already mentioned, small enough to be used in the lowest level. They were described as being 33 ft long by 4 ft beam with a draught of 2 ft. The much larger boats of the north–south section of the main level were referred to as 'M' boats and were 50 ft long, 6 ft 4 in. wide below and 7 ft beam above and had a depth of 2 ft 10 in. The third type of boat was used in the side canals of the main level and was called the narrow boat. Approximately the same length as the 'M' boat, it had a beam of only 4 ft 8 in.

It was only the 'M' boats with their full loads that were brought out of the mines into Worsley Delph. There they were linked up three abreast. Three such groups carrying ninety to one hundred tons in all were towed by a pair of horses into Manchester, taking perhaps five hours over the journey. When this is compared with the previous packhorse travel it is easy to see how the price could be reduced and coal become the driving power for the rapidly expanding industries and the fuel for homes.

The movement of boats within the mines was also described fully. There was a certain amount of legging, the men lying on their backs and walking the tunnel roof. In places there were rings which could be grasped with the help of a short boathook. The most ingenious method, however, was the use of the sluices already mentioned. A group of 'M' boats, filled during the day shift, were collected together, with the sluices closed throughout. These were then opened one by one in succession, and the slight current of about half a mile an hour was enough to carry the whole fleet out into Worsley Delph, where they were timed to arrive at about four o'clock in the morning! There they were met by the horses and the empty boats were waiting to be legged back in the now still waters. As they passed back through the sluices, each was dropped to collect the head of water for the next night's current.

The slight current and the movement of the boats was said to keep the mine clear of gas, and the men worked by candle light. Two small jets of gas issued from fissures, one near the entrance and the other above the inclined plane, and these were lighted. They gave little light but formed landmarks for the halers working the boats.

The whole description, given scientifically and in a low key, paints a mental picture of a vast underworld where journeys must have seemed endless in almost total darkness and where a wrong turning might condemn a haler to wander, lost, through corridors of time. The underground waters, silent except for the splash of occasional drips, must have seemed to run right to the earth's centre.

A visit to the underground canals in the late 1960s started at the Coal Board offices at Walkden. Arrangements had been made for four of us to go down a shaft from the surface and we were duly frisked for matches and issued with hard hats. We then entered a lift cage and were lowered down to the main level. The shaft we used was a short distance only from the famous inclined plane, and we walked to the foot of it by the light of our helmet torches. The plane itself was in perfect condition, a preserved fossil beneath the ground, cool and dry with no light, no rain or frost and no human to deface it. The rails had gone, but the evenly sloping bed of grit was as fresh as the day it was cleaved nearly two hundred years before. We walked up the steep one-in-four slope to the upper canal, the water now very low, leading from the two locks. The locks themselves were missing, but we could see where the great drum had been placed and could follow the channel where the water had flowed from the emptying sluices. On a rock wall several people had carved their names, but we looked in vain for John \Gilbert, James Brindley or the duke.

A canal junction beneath the ground, Worsley, 1963

We retraced our steps and went aboard a waiting starvationer. Our two guides were combining our visit with their own inspection tour of the main canal, which was still used for drainage and was regularly examined for roof falls or blockages. The waters of the channel were stained a deep brownish red by the ochre from the mines, and in the still waters this formed a muddy ooze. Our guides told us that unless they kept up their regular trips with the boat the canal would soon silt up completely and become unnavigable. They told us that there was so much ochre deposited in the channel that many people had considered that it would be worth extracting commercially.

We climbed into the wooden boat and made ready for our journey. My main impression was of the deepest silence so far beneath the ground, broken only by the occasional dripping of water from the roof. We could picture the long strings of loaded boats sliding forward

The Worsley mines boats in Worsley Delph, about 1890

gently with the current as each sluice was raised until eventually they floated out into the Delph where the air was cold beneath the stars.

Our guides pushed off and propelled the boat with short shafts along the walls or roof and occasionally used the toes of their boots when the roof was low. Much of the tunnel was bricked but was unlined where hard rock outcropped. Mostly we could sit up, and our torches sent long beams into the side canals, but occasionally the roof came low and we had to lie full length as the sides of the boat grated the brickwork. At the junctions with the side canals the roof was high and vaulted with beautiful brick arching.

At last we came to a landing place where another shaft came down from the surface and there we left the boat to ride up to the surface. Back in daylight, the underworld seemed quite unreal but I have always been thankful for the experience of exploring the canals which

Worsley Delph today

were shortly to be closed for ever. The last colliery to be drained by the canals has now been closed and barriers have been built inside the tunnel mouths to raise the water level up to the roof in places and to seal in any gas that might collect.

Our actual trip was made some distance from the exits, but had we had more time we could have cruised right out into the Delph. This used to be the repository of many sunken starvationers, and photographs show them lying side by side across the whole of the basin. Some years ago the basin was cleared and the boats were removed and broken up. In 1969, however, when the water level in the tunnel was raised, four boats in good condition were found and two were pulled out and lifted on to the side. One was given to Frank Mullineux of Monks Hall Museum, Eccles, and the other was offered to me at Manchester Museum. The two were slightly different in size, the Eccles one being 36 ft long and ours only 30 ft. Ours had a beam of 3 ft 8 in. and was 2 ft deep, and both were clearly the tub boats of Fournel and Dyévre. Ours is very strongly built, with a double-skinned bottom, the lower skin of inch-thick boards running crosswise and the upper skin, $1\frac{1}{2}$ in. thick, running the length of the boat. It is pointed at both ends and the sides are two planks high. The lower planks consist of two pieces joined in the middle, but the upper planks are single pieces of wood skilfully curved at the ends to meet accurately. Throughout the whole length inside are ribs at 2 ft intervals, giving the craft great strength. The boat weighs approximately a ton and is built of oak throughout. It is, perhaps, one of the oldest boats to be constructed for a branch of the English canal system.

5

The Manchester, Bolton and Bury Canal

The history of this canal is told comprehensively by Tomlinson[43] and by Hadfield and Biddle.[15] It was a canal which might have had important links both with Liverpool and across the Pennines, but these never materialised. Nevertheless, with coal occurring beneath much of its length, and the cotton mills of the Croal and Irwell valleys, it had a quiet and relatively successful history. The idea of such a canal seems to have originated in Bolton in 1790, and Matthew Fletcher, who managed collieries along its route, made the first survey. Hugh Henshall, Brindley's brother-in-law, carried out a further survey and an Act was obtained in 1791. A number of directors were closely concerned with the Mersey and Irwell, for such a canal linking with their navigation could not fail to attract extra trade.

The original line was to be built with narrow locks, and care was taken to plan the supply of water so that it would not affect the many mills on the rivers. A start was made at Oldfield Road, Salford, some little distance from the agreed junction, and the canal was cut westwards and also along the two branches to Bolton and Bury.

At this time the Rochdale canal supporters were trying unsuccessfully to obtain an Act to build their canal across the Pennines. The Manchester, Bolton and Bury directors recalled Brindley's first surveys, one of which was to link the Calder and Hebble navigation in Yorkshire to Manchester through Bury. They tried to promote their own extensions, first to join the Rochdale canal and later to continue to Sowerby Bridge. Eventually, in 1794, the Rochdale was successful with its Act and the extension from Bury failed.

The Manchester, Bolton and Bury directors also hoped to extend their canal westwards from Bolton. At that time the Leeds and Liverpool canal was still being built and its intended line was to run through Red Moss, a few miles only from Bolton, before dropping down thirty locks to Wigan. They approached the Leeds and Liverpool directors to find out whether the Red Moss line was likely to be followed, and received an encouraging reply. At the Leeds and Liverpool's suggestion, they determined to convert their canal to barge width even though this meant rebuilding locks already completed. This would have allowed the same boats to use the two navigations together. In addition they bought land at Red Moss so as to be ready to extend at the earliest possible moment. This too was not to be, for the Leeds and Liverpool eventually chose a different line, locking down at Johnson's Hillock to the southern length of the Lancaster canal, which had a route to Wigan at a rather lower level. From there a branch was built to Leigh to join the Bridgewater, cutting out the Manchester, Bolton and Bury completely. When this happened the directors gave up hope of further extensions and sold their land at Red Moss. Perhaps it was as well, for the water-starved Leeds and Liverpool would have been faced with two long flights of wide locks at Red Moss instead of the one at Aspull.

Though the canal was completed from Oldfield Road to both Bolton and Bury in 1796, no attempt had been made to link up with the Irwell, where six further locks were needed. One scheme envisaged the carrying of the canal over the Irwell, and notice was given of a Bill to Parliament, but this was withdrawn, as it would have met with great opposition. The directors discussed a link with the Rochdale canal by a tunnel from the Irwell, and this idea was revived in 1836 to become the Manchester and Salford Junction Canal. They finally bought land north of Hampson Street and made the river connection in 1808.

Despite the usual take-over or amalgamation with a railway company, in this case the Manchester and Leeds railway, the canal continued to carry coal until well into this century. Many of the earlier coal mines were worked out, but others were sunk sufficiently close to the canal to make full use of it. Unfortunately the subsidence which so often occurs in mining areas, together with the fact that almost throughout its length the canal nestled into a steep valley side, caused serious slips, breaches and bursts. So serious had these been that the Transport Minister ordered the dewatering of a section at Clifton during the last war in case a bomb should cause serious flooding in the valley. The water was never put back, and section by section the canal was abandoned until in 1961 it was legally no more.

Carriage of coal on this canal was similar in pattern to that on the Bridgewater. Slightly shortened, primitive narrow boats were built with boxes which could be lifted in and out at the coal staithes and wharfs. The bottoms of the boxes were made in two halves, hinged downwards and held in place by chains. When lifted out by crane they could be positioned over bunkers or carts and the coal neatly deposited where it was needed. This early form of containerisation speeded loading and unloading to such a degree that canal carrying over short hauls remained competitive in speed as well as in economy.

Meanwhile one other small canal was built to link up with the Manchester, Bolton and Bury at Clifton, west of Prestwich. This was Fletcher's canal, named after Matthew Fletcher, built under a clause allowing cuts to be made to coal mines and quarries.[14] The main canal was to cross the river Irwell at Clifton and continue north-westwards along the north slope of the valley. Fletcher's canal was built to take a parallel course on the south side and to extend for a mile and a half to service the collieries in that area.

As early as the 1750s Brindley had been called in to devise a novel method of draining the Wet Earth colliery at Clifton. This included a waterwheel, powered by the Irwell, and a half-mile channel from the colliery. In 1760 Fletcher extended the channel eastwards to a new mine which was being sunk. About 1790, when Fletcher was one of the active promoters of the Manchester, Bolton and Bury canal, he deepened and widened the channels so that they could be used for the carriage of coal by boat as well as for drainage. The cut was linked to the main canal by a lock 90 ft long and 21 ft wide, with a fall of 18 in.

After the pattern of the Bridgewater canal at Worsley, at least two navigable canals were driven into the hillside. The Wet Earth colliery was worked out in 1928 and all carriage on the canal finished from that date.

We are fortunate in being able to look at the canal in the last century through the eyes of Corbett,[7] who used to row occasionally on both the top and the main length. He also rambled on the towpath of the top pound past collieries, boat-loading tipplers, waterwheels and other structures which the men in charge said were designed by either Brindley or Fulton. Brindley had been dead for twenty years when the canal was first opened but Fulton may have left his influence in the area, for he had proposed an inclined plane instead of the Prestolee locks, with a waterwheel providing the motive power.

Prestolee in the 1850s was a busy manufacturing district with paper works and cotton-spinning mills close to the river. Rowing eastwards from the aqueduct, scullers had to pass a pair of locks at Ringley and another pair at Giant's Seat amongst beautiful woodlands a mile farther on. By the headland of Giant's Seat was 'Old Margaret's Gardens' or 'Barlow's Gardens', which formed a good mooring for

Ringley: the Manchester, Bolton and Bury canal above the river Irwell, 1917

substantial egg teas. There was also Kilcoby Cottage, where tea was served, and this was a popular camping ground. A stream flowed through Nuttall Wood with water so pure that bathers formed the Agecroft Swimming Club as a branch of the rowing club. Eventually, before the turn of the century, the beauty was destroyed by the encroaching spoil of the Oakwood brickworks. When this happened, the Agecroft Rowing Club rented Giant's Seat House with its gardens and orchards and members stayed for weekends or longer. This too had to be relinquished, as it was required by the brickworks manager. They returned to 'Old Meg's Gardens' to find the grounds neglected and much of the beauty gone.

Tea was also obtainable at Rhodes lock, and beyond this the Clifton aqueduct carried the canal across the river past Pilkington's Lancastrian Pottery and the Chloride Electric Accumulator Works. This was described as a 'high class modern business beneficial to the workpeople of the district though not to the foliage'.

Even here the canal had not left open country, for fields and wooded banks extended for another mile. On this length the scullers would sometimes set sail when the wind was in the right quarter. The Cliften Hall collieries with their canal docks occupied an area of extensive coal working, and the subsidence associated with this had often to be counteracted by raising the canal banks, towpaths and bridges. There was one further rural and wooded stretch past Agecroft Hall, with 'large masses of yellow iris bearing numerous flowers'. Beyond were the Agecroft Hall and the deep Pendleton collieries and, as Agecroft Rowing Club men, they would lift their boats out and place them on boat trucks to be wheeled a few hundred yards to the boathouse on the river bank. Corbett's photographic illustrations show a fine, wide canal running mostly through attractive scenery.

The lowermost lengths of the canal are a sorry sight today. It joined the Irwell just north of and almost under Princes Bridge, whose parapet is much too high to allow it to be seen. It can, however, be viewed from a small private property on the south side. The towpath bridge over the entrance has gone and the locks have been entirely eliminated, but the bridge foundations are still visible. The line can be followed on waste ground towards Oldfield Road where it crossed beneath the railway. West of Oldfield Road are Canal Street and Upper Wharf Street, but the basins have been filled in and there is nothing to see. The canal then continued on the north side of the railway and can be seen in places from the Manchester to Bolton train, beautifully built throughout with dressed stone sides and a firm towpath.

The Clifton aqueduct carries the canal across the Irwell, whose valley has narrowed to a rocky gorge. The three arches are of red brick but the rest of the structure is stone. The junction with Fletcher's canal is on the south side but both canals are without water and are largely filled in. There is a sharp turn and a wide basin on the north side, and once more the high quality of construction is apparent. The canal continues westwards through the large sewage farm and is filled in the whole way. It is crossed by the M62 motorway and runs parallel to an abandoned railway which has been turned into an attractive nature trail.

Through the picturesque village of Ringley the canal is scarcely visible, though its course can be followed, and it first appears in water north of Kearsley Road amongst low woodlands. Just beyond the seventh milestone, half hidden in the undergrowth, were the double locks, though now only the top end of the upper lock is visible. The canal continues in water from this point to the junction of the rivers Croal and Irwell at Prestolee, the two rivers flowing in gorges from west and east respectively.

The canal crosses the Irwell on a beautiful four-arched aqueduct, with the arches built once more of red brick and the rest of the structure of stone. It then turns sharply to the right, widening into a basin as it does so, and ascends the north side of the valley by six locks in two staircases of three. The total rise is 66 ft and the slope is impressive. The locks have been filled in but the masonry sides are visible throughout, with little stone steps down on each side. At the top there is a wide turning basin, and this forms the junction of the Bolton and Bury lengths, the former in water and the latter filled in for the first half-mile. Interesting buildings at the junction stand boldly on the hilltop, and milestones are to be found at the bottom marking M(anchester) $7\frac{3}{4}$ and at the top M 8.

Prestolee aqueduct over the Irwell

This area and much of the top length are well described by Mrs L.
Millward,[30] who draws attention to Seddon's Fold at the bottom, an
old farmhouse with disused weaving sheds. She also considers that the
little filled-in arm which ran beneath a bridge at the bottom of the
locks linked with a dry dock which could certainly have been emptied
into the Croal.

At the top, the length from Bolton is up to seventy feet wide and full
of deep, clear water. It runs westwards so close to the steep valley side

Milestone on the Manchester, Bolton and Bury canal

of the Croal that the towpath has been built approximately twenty-five feet wide to retain it. The water is now under the care of an anglers' federation, and the edge of the towpath is painted with numbers for fishing matches. The Croal valley itself has been landscaped and trees planted, and a housing estate reaches nearly to the north bank of the canal.

About a mile west of Prestolee a road sweeps down into the valley in a slight declivity which used to be crossed by the Damside aqueduct, a sturdy structure similar in design to the two already described. This has now gone, and the canal terminates with a small arm swinging north up the valley. Across the road to the west it is possible to pick up the line of the canal again. The whole of the ground has been bulldozed and the channel filled in, but the edge of the towpath is clearly visible and can be followed for a further mile to Darcy Lever. At this point a fourth aqueduct used to carry the canal over both the road and the river Tonge, a tributary of the Croal, but this too has been demolished. Both this and Damside proved exceedingly difficult to destroy when charges were placed in appropriate places and detonated. A loud explosion was accompanied by a pall of smoke and dust, and when this had cleared the aqueduct was seen to be standing as before, practically undamaged! Five months were to elapse before they were both removed, so strongly had they been built.

A short length of towpath can be found west of Darcy Lever and the line can be followed beneath the railway viaduct. The last half-mile and the terminus basin with its wharfs and warehouses have all disappeared before the path of a motorway.

Eastwards of Prestolee it is possible to follow the canal for the whole of its length to Bury. It runs high up on the valley side overlooking the Irwell, and the first two miles towards Radcliffe are extremely beautiful. It is immediately obvious why the canal was filled in from Prestolee, as a major breach had occurred a quarter of a mile along in 1942. At this point the whole canalside has slipped away down into the valley, and the breach is now overgrown with saplings. Beyond the breach there are cracks in the ground parallel to the valley side, and it is easy to appreciate the problems of the builders and maintenance engineers throughout the canal's existence. Coal measures outcrop in the steep valley side, and these consist of massive sandstones and soft shales impervious to water. The subsidence due to the extraction of the coal beneath has started the movement in the more slippery shales. Farther to the west the massive sandstones of Nob End predominate, and these have been quarried as building stones for many of the canal structures.

East of the breach a paper works has been built across the canal, but a little farther along it is in water again. The last colliery to be worked alongside the canal was at Ladyshore, and a few derelict buildings still stand by the canalside with their box boats waiting empty and sunk. Dr Boucher[2] described the scene within forty-eight hours of its being closed, the seams having been worked out. At that time the basin was full of boats and there was a boat-building shed with a narrow boat slipped on to the side, being replanked. The boats were loaded direct from screens, and they carried coal to both Radcliffe and Bury. They were worked in pairs by horse with one man only in charge who prodded them out from time to time, either at the bows or at the stern, using a long shaft. The buildings, the engine house and the offices were all standing but silent; when he returned a year later most had been demolished.

Milestones with their beautifully chiselled numbers were placed at each quarter-mile and tolls could be worked out with great accuracy. This was important, as many of the hauls were quite short, to factories and mills along the canalside. One such stands half a mile east of Ladyshore in the valley below, and its coal bunker still lies some twenty feet below the level of the towpath. A steam crane stands in a little bay beside the towpath, and it is easy to imagine it swinging out over the canal and lifting the coal, box by box, from the moored boat. With each load it could swivel round so that the box hung directly over the bunker and deposit the coal where it was needed. The crane, now very rusty, stands as a silent monument to the days when the mines were worked and the canal was still navigable.

As the canal nears Radcliffe the condition deteriorates and, though the towpath is marked as a public footpath, little is done to keep it clear of rubbish. The main road bridge has been dropped and the canal runs beneath in a small pipe. It is in water for two more miles to Bury, passing the very attractive 'Farmer's Arms', which used to have its own small wharf and winding hole – a widened section where boats could turn. The quality of construction of this length is most striking, the towpath cobbled and stone-sided throughout. Fences are formed of flagstones set on edge and linked with iron bolts connecting diamond-shaped plates on either side.

The canal passes through James Crompton's paper works and into an area south of the Bury-to-Bolton road by Irwell Bridge. Here the

Canalside crane for lifting coal boxes from the boats and swinging them over to coal bunkers

basins with their surrounding warehouses used to lie, but all is now levelled for redevelopment. Boucher described the basins when they were still receiving coal. A steam crane ran on a central platform between the two arms and lifted out the boxes to carry them to waiting lorries. At Crompton's the boxes were lifted out by an overhead runway and carried direct into the boilerhouse. All this finished when Ladyshore became worked out.

Crompton's had an unusual icebreaker, the *Sarah Lansdale*, which they have donated to the Boat Museum at Ellesmere Port. This is slightly narrower than the standard narrow boat, with a flat, sloping stem and two rails one along each side for the crew to hold on to. When the ice thickened on the canal in winter, the boat was towed by a team of horses while the crew, standing with their legs apart, rocked it from side to side. The boat was of sturdy construction and would ride up on to the ice and break through it. There are stories, however, of ice being so thick that the boat would be dragged right out on to its surface and would skate along until it could be halted!

A short extension of the canal crossed beneath the main road, now a roundabout, in a small-bore tunnel, to reappear on the north side between small wharfs and warehouses. This was a narrow navigable feeder from the Irwell, available to supply water only when it overtopped a certain level. Millers in the Irwell valley were most suspicious of the canal, and great care had to be taken to ensure that no water was taken when levels were low. It was the same millers who had to be placated when the extension through Haslingden to Church on the Leeds and Liverpool canal was being considered. Lifts instead of locks were to have been built, but the canal was never started.

Even though the Manchester, Bolton and Bury canal is now no longer navigable, it is well worth a visit both for its scenery and for a study of its construction. It was a high-quality canal, well built, but one that suffered greatly from subsidence. Its methods of working are of special interest, particularly the containerisation of the box boats. And, in time, the Croal and Irwell valleys may regain something of their former beauty.

6

The Rochdale Canal

The background history of the Rochdale canal is fully covered by Hadfield and Biddle.[15] It is a long history with many ups and downs but it ended with the completion of one of the best-built canals in the country. The final result was a wide canal with barge locks long enough to take a pair of full-length narrow boats, and it crossed the Pennines without a single major tunnel. Such a canal proved expensive to build, and it was never able to pay the high dividends of other canals which had needed less capital. When fully maintained, however, it could carry greater loads than most other canals of its time. Mr Reginald Wood, son of Albert Wood, the principal carrier on the Rochdale canal seventy years ago, told me that it was possible with careful loading to carry as much as seventy tons across the Pennines in certain of their boats.

In 1766, when the Leeds and Liverpool canal was first being considered, a number of gentlemen met in the Union Flag inn, Rochdale, to discuss a link between the Calder and Hebble in Yorkshire and either the Mersey and Irwell navigation or the Bridgewater canal. James Brindley was asked to carry out two surveys, one on the present course and the other through Bury, both to include Rochdale. The Leeds and Liverpool went ahead even though fifty years were to pass before it was fully opened, but no action was taken on the Rochdale.

In 1790 and 1791 the scheme was revived, and further surveys were carried out by John Rennie and William Crossley, Senior. Two hundred thousand pounds was raised in record time even though there was great competition with the subscribers to the Manchester, Bolton and Bury canal, who had a number of rival extension schemes, including links across the Pennines and with the Leeds and Liverpool canal. It was hoped to link the Rochdale with the Mersey and Irwell or the Bridgewater, but the duke refused to allow a junction to be made. Several of the Mersey and Irwell directors were themselves interested in the Manchester, Bolton and Bury and there was little enthusiasm for the Rochdale there. A Bill was sent to Parliament in 1792 but it failed to get sufficient support.

There was much discussion as to whether the canal should be built with narrow or wide locks, and it was realised that if it was built wide it would cost a lot more money. It would, however, be joining two wide navigations, and there were clearly advantages in constructing it to full barge width. However, in 1793 a second Bill was sent to Parliament for a narrow canal with a 3,000-yard tunnel at the summit. On this occasion the company had obtained the duke's support, which he gave subject to a very large compensation toll to be paid on all traffic from the Rochdale except flagstones. He was later to cut this to a third before the canal was completed. It was supposed to offset the money he made from warehousing and wharfage of goods being transported by land carriage across the Pennines. Perhaps also he realised that the rival Manchester, Bolton and Bury schemes would cut out his own canal. This Bill failed by one vote only.

William Jessop was called in for consultation and he proposed a wide canal which would not need a tunnel if the summit level was raised to a greater height by a further series of seven locks on each side. The new line formed the basis of a third Bill in 1794 which was successful, and work started immediately. The thirty-three miles were to include ninety-two locks, and the total cost eventually exceeded £600,000. The top levels were so short that they had to be made wider and deeper to act as reservoirs, and the locks, except those below Dale Street, were made to have a ten-foot rise and interchangeable gates. The two sides were open by 1799, but money problems held up the completion of the section between Todmorden and Rochdale, which was not opened until 1804. Nevertheless, though the last to start, the

Rochdale was the first canal to be completed across the Pennines.

Priestley[35] commented that such a canal would link the two seas on either side of England for vessels to pass from the one to the other and for goods to come direct from the Baltic to Liverpool and other Lancashire towns. He glossed over the different depths and lock

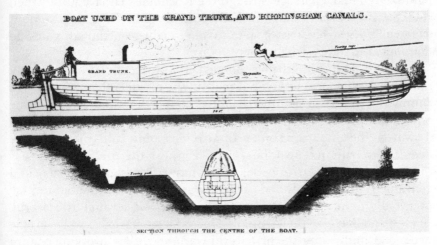

A narrow boat of 1826; after Strickland. The Grand Trunk is the Trent and Mersey canal

Contemporary model of the directors' boat, Rochdale Canal Co., in Rochdale Museum. The model is 30½ in. long, 6 in. wide and 5½ in. high; probably 1/24 scale

lengths of the two canals, for the Calder and Hebble was built for shorter boats of greater draught. The North Western Museum of Inland Navigation owns the Yorkshire 'West Country' keel *Ethel*, built for the coal trade on the Calder and Hebble. Though only 57 ft long, she still carried seventy tons but would have had to be considerably lightened to make passage through the Rochdale. To save water when such boats crossed the Pennines, the locks over the Rochdale summit were built with recesses for gates at fifty-eight feet, though gates do not appear to have been fitted.

Hadfield and Biddle give details of a successful but relatively uneventful existence throughout most of the nineteenth century, when commercial carriage kept at a fairly high level, though tolls came down sharply in the 1840s with competition from the railways. Towards the end, tonnage was also dropping and the company decided to run its own boats to keep up the traffic. This was discontinued, but many boatmen hired or bought boats and continued to trade. Albert Wood was such a boatman, and he eventually built up a fleet of over fifty boats, based first at Sowerby Bridge and later at the Ashton's Ducie Street basin as well. Traffic declined rapidly after the first world war and the last working boat to make the through trip finished in 1937.

Many of the subsequent events have been described by Boucher.[2] By the late 1940s all traffic had finished except on the short length through Manchester. A Bill of abandonment had been considered but was not sent to Parliament until 1952. At that time the councils of both Manchester City and Lancashire County wished to demolish road overbridges and replace them at a lower level, and the Bill was accepted. The whole canal from Dale Street to Sowerby Bridge was abandoned to navigation, and only the mile and a quarter in the city centre remained.

Unfortunately for the people along its course, an Act of abandonment does not remove the canal. The lowering of bridges, the culverting of sections and the construction of buildings across its bed merely cut the canal into a series of short lengths. In the country these can retain their beauty and become true haunts of nature, but in towns they degenerate into rubbish dumps. This undoubtedly happened at the western end, and drownings occurred, with children making a dangerous no-man's-land into their playground. In particular the people of Newton Heath suffered, as there was little playground space in their densely built-up area and the children were attracted to the canalside. Manchester City Council considered possible ways of ensuring greater safety and finally determined on a half-million-pound scheme of filling in the canal except for the final few inches and laying a level bed from side to side. The locks were also filled in and their tails stepped down to the lower level. Such a shallow channel could still deliver water, though neither anglers nor boats could use it. This work was completed in 1971 from Great Ancoats Street for two and a half miles to the city boundary.

Meanwhile the mile and a quarter from Castlefield to Dale Street remained navigable and was in good order as late as 1953. In 1955 the North West Electricity Board in Dickinson Street changed from coal to oil and the two little arms were filled in. Shortly after this the salt from Middlewich ceased to be carried to the salt warehouse in Dale Street and commercial traffic was virtually at an end. A few pleasure boats came through, but they had to pay a toll of 15s, and as maintenance lapsed the journey became more difficult. Boucher noted that the condition was poor in 1959, worse in 1960 and in 1961 forty-eight hours' notice had to be given and the canal used from Monday to Friday only and in the short period between ten o'clock and two o'clock. It was at this point that I personally became involved.

If the canal was to be kept open, it must be shown by a boat to be still navigable. The company could see no future for it as a navigation, especially as the Ashton canal was practically unnavigable and there seemed no possibility of restoration. It was known that the company was likely to seek an Act of abandonment so that the whole length in the city could be redeveloped. If this was not successfully opposed, a link in the chain of the Cheshire ring of canals would be broken and soon other lengths would be lost.

We therefore brought the narrow boat *Parrot* to the bottom lock at Castlefield and arranged for it to collect some spoil which had to be removed from a building site seven locks up. We were within our rights to request a passage, as the canal was still legally navigable, and this was granted. We faced extreme difficulties in making the journey, which took twelve days to cover the mile and a quarter to the junction with the Ashton canal. The details were described in my *Water rallies*.[33] The following year, in 1965, the company agreed to retain the navigation of this section as long as the Ashton remained legally open. This was written into their Bill which they sent to Parliament.

Five years later the company suggested a rally of boats in Manchester and asked the Inland Waterways Association and the Peak Forest Canal Society to take on the organisation. A great deal of maintenance and repair work needed to be carried out, for the condition of the locks and channel had deteriorated. The Peak Forest Canal Society working parties agreed to do all they could to make the canal usable.

Throughout the winter the company co-operated closely, making their offices available for meetings. They nominated their engineer to represent them on the organising committee and provided materials for the actual repairs whenever possible. Weekend after weekend, the working parties climbed into the locks, removed the rubbish, replanked the gates where the timber had shrunk or rotted and replaced paddle gear which had been removed to prevent mischief. They faced many problems, the worst occurring under the newly completed Rodwell Tower. The bottom gates of this lock were in a state of collapse and the volunteers rebuilt them, strapping them together with steel rods purchased as scrap from abandoned railways.

The weekend after Easter was chosen for the rally, as this would allow the volunteers time for an all-out final effort. One hundred and three boats made the journey safely to Dale Street and into the bottom basin of the Ashton canal, and all returned safely after the event. The Lord Mayor of Manchester and mayors and chairmen of neighbouring towns, together with a director and the manager of the Rochdale Canal Company, went aboard and cruised beneath Rodwell Tower. They disembarked in the basin and the Lord Mayor made a speech looking forward to the time when the whole Cheshire ring of canals would be open again.

After this successful rally no more trips were made, and the canal began to deteriorate once more. On several locks new gates were needed, and it was hoped that these would be in position by the time the Ashton canal was restored and reopened. Though all were not replaced by June 1975, the company agreed to make it possible for boats to use the canal *en route* for Dukinfield at the junction of the Ashton and Peak Forest canals. A rally of boats had been organised, and we decided to make the journey from Marple through to Manchester and the Bridgewater. It was an exciting day, for we started early from Fairfield top lock after the rally had finished and reached the Ducie Street bridge between the two canals before midday. A number of craft, including two beautifully restored boats from the North Western Museum of Inland Navigation, were waiting in the Dale Street basin and Peak Forest volunteers were working them carefully through.

When our turn came we entered the top lock with two other boats and quickly descended and nosed into the darkness beneath Rodwell Tower. Part of this building stands on concrete columns which rise out of the water and restrict the channel so that two boats are not quite able to pass abreast. We had been warned not to bump the gates in the tower lock, as they were a hundred years old and very fragile, but all went well and we were soon through the tunnel which passes under Piccadilly. We cruised on beside Canal Street, which is still the official towpath although it is lined with cars and parking meters! Perhaps one day a horse-drawn boat will come through and take the tops off all the meters.

At Princess Street the towpath crosses the canal on its own little footbridge beside the busy main road and continues along the south side of the canal. From here onwards the route lies between tall buildings or high walls until it joins the Bridgewater, giving a strange feeling of isolation in the centre of the city. The towpath is no longer a right of way. Below Oxford Street the water began to build up and overflow on to the towpath. The next lock is just below the entrance of the extensive but now filled-in basins which used to lead to the Manchester and Salford Junction canal (p. 98). The canal then runs between red sandstone walls which mark the site of a tunnel opened out early in the last century. Three sunken barges lie along the side opposite the towpath, their condition too far gone to permit restoration. The rectangular Roman fort of Mamucium lay across the ground over the tunnel, and when this was opened a number of Roman objects were found. A small piece of the wall still stands beneath railway arches near the final lock. Some of the finds, together with maps and plans of the fort which commanded the fording of the Irwell, are on show in Manchester Museum.

The last lock at Castle Street is also hewn out of red sandstone and brings the canal down to the Bridgewater level; the junction is a few yards only beyond it.

This had been a beautifully built canal. The stonework of the locks is good and the massive granite masonry forming the sills is as unworn today as it was when first laid in place. It is a pity that the overflows (or 'by-washes') have been filled in, but when these have been renewed throughout there will be few problems in making the trip through the centre of the city.

A walk up the abandoned length of the Rochdale canal is a sad and disheartening experience. It is not possible to reach the canalside between Dale Street car park and Great Ancoats Street. The great salt warehouse still stands in the car park, though the canal branch to it has been filled in and the huge canal warehouse used by Hall and Rogers is also without its water connections. The canal can be seen both from Leech Street and on the south side of Great Ancoats Street, and is a linear rubbish dump with a trickle of water running through.

North of this street it is possible to follow the canal for several miles except for a short length by Coleshill Street. Redhill Street acted as the canal towpath as far as North Union Street bridge, a roving bridge which carried the towpath across to the south side and through a small separate tunnel. From here the towpath has been asphalted, lamps have been sited, trees planted and grass laid wherever there was sufficient space. For the whole length as far as the city boundary by Brook Street and Stotts Lane the canal flows on a flat bed only inches below the surface. The locks on this stretch are numerous, and all have been filled in and given a channel again only inches deep. The lower end consists of a series of steps and much of the water disappears into pipes and reappears at the bottom. Council estates line the canal from the old bridge at Butler Street northwards for a few hundred yards, and it is clear that the building of such estates close to a canal is questionable. If it is navigable it needs supervision to prevent drownings. The same is even more true if it is derelict, for few adults are likely to go near it. Such a shallow channel as this is clearly one answer, though the bottom becomes dirty and slippery and it needs two gardeners working regularly on it to keep it clear of mud, slime and rubbish.

Between Varley Street and Hulme Hall Road the canal towpath is closed to the public. Farther east the towpath is regained and a notice announces 'Rochdale Canal Park'. For some distance there are low industrial buildings on either side and then the large engineering works of Mather and Platt. Beyond this, in Newton Heath, the land is derelict on both banks and the channelled canal with its narrow grass verge and small trees struggling for survival is completely without character. The water is clean and clear but too shallow for anything larger than the smallest tiddlers. This is all that is left of the once great Rochdale canal, without boats, without anglers and apparently without much future, for it is now the stream that no one really wants.

Beyond the city boundary the untreated derelict canal starts again. The water is deep and surprisingly clear, and every item of rubbish can be seen. Whole cars are beneath the surface and baths, mattresses, mowing machines and articles of junk of every kind are visible, particularly within the lock chambers. These have had concrete walls built in place of the top gates, and rubbish lies packed against them with water trickling through. Once more there is derelict land, but many of the great mills remain, giving the dead navigation a feeling of authenticity.

Clear of the towns, the canal passes through countryside of great beauty, particularly near its summit at Littleborough and Todmorden. Here its wide, deep stretches lying between high, heather-covered moors are more like a string of small highland lakes.

The Rochdale Canal Society are examining the possibility of eventual complete restoration of the canal, a large, expensive but not impossible task. Already they are having some success in the country stretches, and they have also assessed the major problems. When this is achieved, it would perhaps be better to cut a short link to Hollinwood and to restore the Hollinwood arm to the main Ashton canal. This would allow the shallowed channel to be obliterated, to the satisfaction of most of the people who live by its side. It would also give the Rochdale canal a much more attractive course and better access to Manchester, though it would restrict navigation to boats of not more than 7 ft beam.

7

The Ashton and Peak Forest Canals

The background history of these two navigations is fully covered by Hadfield and Biddle[15] and that of the Ashton is also well described by Keaveney and Brown.[23] They are taken together in this chapter, for, though they were built and owned by separate companies, they form a single route from the centre of Manchester to the Pennine hills and their entire history has been very closely linked.

The Ashton was permitted by Act of Parliament in 1792, 'An Act for making a navigable canal from Manchester to or near Ashton-under-Lyne and Oldham in the County Palatine of Lancaster'. At first sight the construction of a canal isolated from the rest of the system may seem strange. It was, however, logical, for important coal mines lay in the environs of Ashton and Oldham. Further, the Rochdale canal had been under discussion for some years and there was little doubt that it was soon to be built. In addition to the probable western link, it was hoped that the east would be joined by a trans-Pennine navigation and this was realised when the Huddersfield canals were completed. The company also made provision for a half-mile branch southwards across the Tame, and this was soon to be joined to the Peak Forest canal, whose Act was to receive royal assent two years later.

The Ashton canal was planned to run mostly on the south side of the river Medlock, with a northern branch at Fairfield towards Oldham. A clause in the Act allowed mine owners to construct their own cuts, which could be as much as four miles long. In 1793 the

Ashton proprietors obtained a second Act, which allowed them to build a branch southwards to Stockport and to extend the northern arm to Hollinwood. From here it was pushed even farther north by the Werneth colliery company under the above clause. This upset the Rochdale Canal Company, who had intended to build a branch to Hollinwood themselves. One further length was built from the Hollinwood arm to Fairbottom, and yet another was planned from the Stockport arm to Beat Bank to serve collieries in the Denton area, but this was never completed.

As with other navigations built at this time, the Ashton ran into many problems and had difficulty in finding a suitable engineer to oversee the project until Benjamin Outram joined them in 1798. This was the period of the 'canal mania' and too much work was available for the few experienced engineers. However, the line was completed between Ancoats and Ashton and up the Hollinwood branch in 1796 and to Stockport the following year. The length down to Piccadilly was open in 1799, with warehouses built round the terminal basin, and the proprietors were deeply concerned that the Rochdale company had not completed their line through Manchester to join the Bridgewater canal. This was actually completed in 1800 and a junction was made which gave them an outlet to the west.

Originally the Ashton proprietors had considered building the Peak Forest themselves but found that they had enough to do with their own project. They gave all possible support to the Bill when it came before Parliament in 1794, for such a navigation would be expected to increase trade on their own. The line was first planned to extend through Hyde and Marple to Chapel Milton, whence a tramway could be laid to the limestone quarries around Dove Holes. A year later it was decided to terminate the canal at Bugsworth and extend the tram route from Chapel Milton down the valley. Benjamin Outram had worked with William Jessop on the Cromford canal and was appointed engineer to the whole project. He was a partner in the Butterley ironworks of Derbyshire and had considerable experience in the building of tramways.

Perhaps the most important shareholder was Samuel Oldknow of Mellor, Marple and Stockport, the cotton genius who pioneered the manufacture of muslin. He is said to have been a good employer and, while his mills absorbed the women and children, he was always on the look-out for suitable work for the menfolk. Masons and carpenters found employment in the construction of the canal and others were needed in the quarries, the limekilns and the small coal mines in the area. Oldknow's chief fault was his inability to manage money, but he found a staunch backer in Richard Arkwright of Cromford, who lent him very considerable sums.

The lower length of the Peak Forest canal was open as far as the Marple aqueduct in 1799 and across the aqueduct and along the entire top length in 1800. Money was scarce, the locks had not yet been built, and Outram laid a tramroad track along the side from the top to the bottom. It continued to be used until 1807 even though money had been raised and the locks were in full operation in 1804.

Both canals had moderate financial success, though neither made huge profits. Both benefited by the opening of the Macclesfield canal in 1831, for this gave access to the Midlands and a shorter route to London. The opening of the Cromford and High Peak railway at the same time also brought in more traffic. However, railway traffic was soon to intervene, and both canals were sold or leased to the Sheffield, Ashton under Lyne and Manchester railway, later to become the Manchester, Sheffield and Lincolnshire, and subsequently the Great Central, in the late 1840s. Their moderate success from that time onwards was due partly to railway rivalry, for these canals together with the Macclesfield extended into other companies' areas, and partly to the fact that stone and lime from the Pennines make fine canal cargoes. In addition to this, Ashton and other towns along the route were expanding and mills were being sited along the navigations, which provided a good supply of water as well as the cheapest method of carrying coal.

Towards the end of the century and in the early nineteen-hundreds both canal maintenance and carriage of goods declined. On the other hand, pleasure boating was encouraged, a most unusual situation among canal companies throughout the land. Westall,[47] writing in 1908, commented, 'The enterprising owners (the Great Central Railway Company) have a most liberal tariff for navigation of their series of three canals – Ashton, Peak Forest and Macclesfield . . . the toll for a motor boat for the forty two miles from end to end being only 8*s* – an object lesson to many other railways and canal companies, who by no means appreciate the potential advantages that may accrue from the use of their, in some instances, moribund waterways by motor boats and for which there is mutual adaptation'; again, 'The Great Central Railway Company encourage pleasure boating on these canals and the tolls charged are merely nominal.' Today the North Cheshire Cruising Club, founded in 1943 and based at High Lane on the Macclesfield canal, is the oldest canal cruising club in the country and one of the largest and most enterprising.

Throughout the last war traffic continued to flow on both the Ashton and Peak Forest canals, but once the war was over it dropped rapidly. After nationalisation in 1948 little or no maintenance was carried out, and it was clear that the Ministry of Transport could see no future for either canal below Marple top lock. The top pound of the Peak Forest and its link with the Macclesfield might be kept open for pleasure boaters with minimum maintenance, for all commercial traffic had ceased by 1958.

In 1961 the Ministry decided to abandon a number of canal links in different parts of the country, and both the Hollinwood and the Stockport lengths were lost at this time. With the writing on the wall for the rest of the Ashton canal, the Inland Waterways Association organised two major events. The first was a rally cruise from Marple top lock through to Manchester. Eight boats took part and had some trouble in the deep Marple locks, but one only made the complete journey down to the Ashton. The night before they were due to reach lock 11, vandals set fire to the gates and dropped them into the bottom. A single boat, *Bruce*, from the Midlands, was lifted out and carried or dragged round to continue the rest of the journey under great difficulties.

The second event was a public meeting in Manchester, with Mr L. Scott of the *Guardian* in the chair. After a number of fighting speeches, a resolution was taken urging the Ministry of Transport to restore the canal to a fully navigable condition. Doubtless this resolution still lies in some civil service file together with other 'lost causes'. However, the canal cause was not to be lost.

The long winter of 1961–62 was very cold indeed, and water seeped into the stonework of the Marple aqueduct, freezing, and pushing out the masonry sides. The actual channel was not affected but the two sides of the whole structure were damaged and weakened. Stop planks were put in at Marple top lock – there had been a notice for some time with a completely erroneous height restriction advising people not to cruise down – and the whole of the lower Peak Forest canal was cut off. It was learned that it would cost £35,000 to repair the aqueduct but £7,000 less to demolish it and carry water across by alternative means.

At this point the council of Bredbury and Romiley stepped in. The town clerk called a meeting of local authorities and everyone interested in the canal and in the magnificent aqueduct. It was agreed that the difference in cost must be found, that the aqueduct must be scheduled as an ancient monument, and that it would not be satisfactory unless it was playing its part on a fully restored canal. All this took time, and the following winter of 1962–63 was the coldest on record for two hundred years. Further damage occurred and a larger sum was needed to cover the repairs, but it was found and the repairs were carried out to a very high standard. In the meantime the Marple locks had not been used and quickly became unusable.

In 1964 a new force appeared with the formation of the Peak Forest Canal Society, whose stated aims were the complete restoration of that canal. Members were prepared to carry out voluntary work on the locks and channel and a deputation went to London to ask permission of the British Waterways Board. I was a member of that deputation and we put our case before the chairman, Sir John Hawton, and some of his colleagues. We were asked if we were also interested in the restoration of the Ashton, and we replied that we would certainly wish to see the whole length from Marple top lock to Castlefield in Manchester fully navigable. We were told that the Board could see little future in the Ashton canal and that if they allowed us to start restoration on the Peak Forest it would be the thin end of the wedge! However, they had no objection to our tidying up the towpath, but we must keep clear of the locks themselves.

So the working party came into being and started to tidy the canal in the Woodley area and to replace a broken and dangerous hand rail in the Woodley tunnel. Before long, against instructions, the working party moved to the Marple locks, first to prevent further deterioration and then to do some restoration. In 1964 a further blow occurred when the aqueduct over Store Street in Manchester was found to leak. The length was closed and emptied, pipes were laid across the aqueduct and all navigation was effectively stopped from entering either end of the two canals.

In 1966 the Inland Waterways Association held their national rally of boats at Marple and on that occasion I was chairman. Thousands of people came to look at the locks, and we had a small boat cruise from the bottom across the now repaired aqueduct to Romiley. The lower Peak Forest canal was in a sorry state, with rubbish beneath the bridges and the tunnel entrances and a great coating of weed across the surface. A solitary angler told me that the canal in this derelict condition was now of little use to fishermen, for the water, even in the gaps between the weed, became lifeless without movement and without oxygen.

Throughout this period the Peak Forest Canal Society's working parties were doing admirable work. They had even purchased second-hand timber to replace broken lock beams and were also mending sluices. Working parties were being formed in other parts of the country and an excellent publication appeared called *Navvies' Notebook*. This was the brainchild of Graham Palmer, and it recorded the various groups with their secretaries' addresses and the programmes of work that they were carrying out. *Navvies' Notebook*, the title shortened to *Navvies*, is now run by the Waterways Recovery Group, who have put voluntary work on an organised basis. They have also collected funds and bought mechanical equipment which is made available to societies competent to use it.

By 1968 the organisation was such that a major operation could be planned and carried out, and the first was scheduled to take place in September on the Ashton canal. Named 'Operation Ashton' or 'Op. Ashton', it was planned to clear rubbish from the top seven locks and their intervening pounds. There was a very real need for this work to be done on the grounds of safety if for no other reason. A few months before, I had walked the locks and had found small children playing *inside* a lock, standing on rubbish and climbing over pools quite deep enough to drown them.

Navvies announced Op. Ashton months in advance, giving details of all arrangements, and, a week before, the Peak Forest working party made all ready and assisted the Board in draining the water away. A headquarters was set up with a canteen marquee, a first aid centre and an office to direct parties to their sites. A hall had been hired for those who would bring their camp bedding, and my wife joined the ladies in preparing a huge stew supper for the hungry multitudes that were expected. We were not disappointed, for six hundred people came in parties from all over the country, from places with canals and places without. When we arrived, we were told, 'Lock 13 – clear out the chamber,' and each group was sent to a particular pitch. As we worked, we were a self-contained group but it was at lunch as we walked up the flight that we were able to meet the visitors from far afield. The work proceeded through a thoroughly wet weekend, but the weather had little effect on people working in muddy water already. In all, two thousand tons of rubbish were shifted and as much as possible was burnt. The rest was carried in dumpers to a central point where hired lorries carted it away to a tip. All this cost money which was subscribed by well-wishers who could not come to the operation and by the volunteers themselves. Where possible, masonry pushed over into the canal was retrieved and volunteer masons and bricklayers repaired the damage. When we had finished and the water was back, the canal was a safer place than before and local people, who had been crying out for it to be filled in, were delighted with our work. There were, of course, a few dissenting voices.

Derelict urban canals are always a problem, and in the case of the Ashton canal a large volume of water was carried and supplied to industry. As early as 1961 it was said that an alternative source of water would cost £3 million if the canal was filled in. Culverting – putting the water in a pipe – was already known to cost comparable sums of money where it had been carried out in Glasgow, Edinburgh and other places. Thus the cheapest as well as the most satisfactory way of maintaining the water supply was to restore the canal to full navigation. We organised a conference in Manchester for local authority representatives and explained the whole situation to them, and the point was duly taken.

Shortly after this, the British Waterways Board under the vigorous and positive chairmanship of Sir Frank Price started talks with the local authorities about the future of both canals. This led eventually to a decision to carry out a complete restoration, with local authorities helping to meet the cost. The Inland Waterways Association donated £10,000 towards the work on the Ashton, and the Peak Forest Canal Society raised £3,000 towards restoration of that canal. They also offered their now very experienced volunteers, whose proud boast is that they climbed into and cleared every lock on the two canals.

This very satisfactory conclusion led to a second major working party organised by *Navvies* and the Peak Forest society. The Board were worried about the problems of dredging the top pound of the Ashton, particularly in the Portland Basin–Guide Bridge area. They asked if volunteers could remove all large objects from this stretch and across the aqueduct on the Peak Forest canal. Once more, Graham Palmer and the working parties assessed the problem, and a late weekend in March 1972 was chosen for 'Ashtac' (Ashton Attack). The whole length was drained, a monorail was laid along the towpath and a thousand volunteers came from far and near to help. Five loading bays were chosen, each with a crane or a land-based grab, and the whole operation was organised with military precision. The rubbish of years in the empty channel looked forbidding, but the volunteers were soon in the mud in their waders, some dragging the old tyres, the timber, the mattresses and mowing machines and objects indescribable or nondescript to the side. Others took over and loaded the monorail trucks, while yet others pushed these to the collecting points. When the weekend was over, the Board's news release stated that nine weeks' work and £15,000 had been saved and 3,000 tons of rubbish removed. The length of the Ashton canal at this point is practically inaccessible to machines, for a high wall separates the railway from the narrow towpath. The 'chinese coolie' system which our numbers allowed us to employ was ideally suited to the situation.

The problems facing the engineers were formidable, for the Ashton had two major aqueducts, both of which leaked, and the Peak Forest ran for much of its course along the hillside, with the ever-present possibility of a serious breach occurring. In addition, vandalism and dumping of rubbish had continued for years. Furthermore their funds and staffs were limited, and men had to be brought from other sections to keep up the time schedule. The work was completed in March 1974 and resulted in an excellent piece of restoration.

All that was now left was an official opening, which took place on 13 May, when the Minister, Mr Denis Howell, unveiled a plaque. In his speech he congratulated the Board, the local authorities and the volunteers and said that the time had now come when we must think, not merely of reopening derelict canals, but of building new ones. The movement of water from the hills to the towns and from the north to the dryer south-east could be achieved better by open canals available for all to use and enjoy than by pipes buried beneath the ground. These heartening words echoed our own thoughts and desires.

We made our first journey by boat twelve days later, at the spring-bank holiday. We travelled down from Marple top to Manchester and back, and were able to confirm the high quality of the restoration, particularly of the once so derelict Ashton canal. Furthermore, the Ashton towpath had been levelled and cleared and the lock sides brightened with turf and trees. The walk is now both attractive and interesting, and the towpath is reached from Dale Street, a few hundred yards north of Piccadilly station.

The main Ashton basin lies to the south of this point, and there are plans to turn it into a marina where boats can find a safe night mooring and people can enjoy the water scene in the centre of a great city.

Walking northwards, the towpath crosses Store Street on the now repaired aqueduct and reaches the first lock. Between this and the second lock at Vesta Street there is a small bridge over the now abandoned Islington branch, which was full of an incredible quantity and variety of rubbish when I last looked. A glance will show that it is an excellent example of the state into which an urban canal can get once navigation is abandoned. At one time there were many similar but shorter branches, most of which have now been filled up. The large-scale survey maps published in the 1840s show a whole series of such arms on both the Ashton and the Rochdale canals, each of which had its group of warehouses or its small dock. These bear witness of the trade which the canals brought into Manchester.

The lock at Vesta Street was the scene of the reopening ceremony and the unveiling of the plaque. After one further lock by Ancoats hospital, the canal runs between a veritable canyon of tall red-brick buildings, including mills and warehouses, and then swings across the Medlock valley to flow above the river and beneath the railway and road at the same point. This is the longest level pound in the whole flight of locks and is terminated by the one shallow lock in the flight. The next locks follow closely as the canal passes Bradford colliery, the cause of considerable subsidence. The Board has a small depot at this point, and the towpath changes sides. Anchor Chemicals and the Ciba Clayton aniline works on the canalside by lock 9 have co-operated with the Board to improve their frontage. The locks at this point are very deep, and the canal rises steeply past the abandoned Stockport branch. The buildings from here as far as Crabtree Lane have been demolished, and wide views of industrial Manchester are seen from the open area. A bridge lifts the towpath over the branch, which terminates so abruptly that it is difficult to follow its original course.

From here the locks are rather more spaced out, and the canal passes under a lift bridge which requires sixty turns of a long handle to raise. This and the swing bridge at Crabtree Lane and a further one beyond require a special key obtained from the lock keeper, as they are secured by handcuff locks to prevent misuse.

The area around the top lock at Fairfield is attractive and interesting. The lock itself is one of a pair, though only one has been restored, and the little stone boathouse below used to hold the packet boat in the days of passenger travel. The stone footbridge has graceful proportions and the lock cottage completes the scene. Just above is the junction with the Hollinwood branch, now a dead end a few yards along. A huge brick mill stands on the corner and the canal bears away to the right.

Fairfield top locks, with the packet boathouse on the left

The three level miles to Portland Basin run past Robertson's 'Golden Shred' works and through an area of pleasant houses and parkland. Two skew brick bridges carry the railway across and, at the second, a road passes over both railway and canal. Beyond Guide Bridge station the railway runs very close to the canal and large mills stand on the north side. These buildings, more than a hundred years old, are examples of the high quality of Victorian workmanship, though so many lie empty today. Some are well maintained but the broken windows of others betoken an uncertain future. A little dock with sufficient room for one narrow boat only was constructed on the south side by the railway company as an interchange for goods passing from rail to water and vice versa.

Portland Basin has still something of its former charm as a canal junction though so much has gone in recent years. First a huge red-brick mill was totally destroyed by fire on the north-east side, then the beautiful Ashton canal warehouse which faced the Tame aqueduct was burnt out even though it was still occupied. Dated 1836, its cranes were operated by a waterwheel driven by water from the canal falling through a channel beneath the canal and into the river Tame. The remains of this wheel are still in position. The stone bridge, also dated

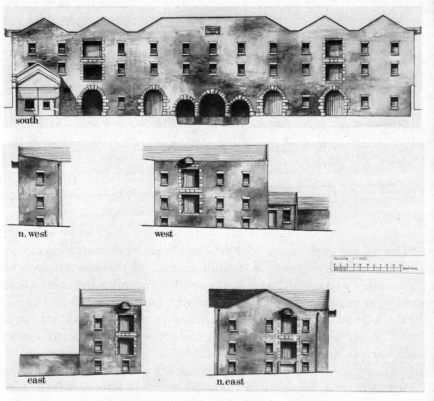

Ashton Canal warehouse, Dukinfield

1836, carrying the towpath across the junction, is similar to that at Fairfield, with equally fine proportions, and there is a little gas lamp post which used to carry the date 1846. The stone-built Tame aqueduct leads off to the south, with a wide towpath on both sides.

The Ashton canal continues for another half-mile to the bottom lock of the Huddersfield Narrow canal, which crossed the Pennines into Yorkshire. This canal and the short length of the Ashton are now derelict, though a society is examining the possibilities of a complete restoration.

Though now abandoned, some lengths of the Hollinwood branch are both interesting and attractive. The first half-mile as far as Medlock Road has been filled in and obliterated. The few hundred yards beyond this have also been filled in, but a path runs down the centre with grass and small trees on either side. The line of the canal is clearly marked from the junction by a succession of red-brick mills built along its banks. The small aqueduct over the railway at Droylsden junction has now gone but the length between Lumb Mill and Cinderland Bridge is surprisingly full of water. Both ends are cut off by concrete walls, but this quarter of a mile is fished by the Moorside anglers.

A further half-mile runs between fields and a golf course and brings the canal to the south side of the Medlock valley. Beyond the road junction of Lumb Lane, Newmarket Road and Cutler Hill Road the towpath becomes public and the canal worth close inspection. The sixty-six-yards-long Waterhouses tunnel, brick-built and with a towpath, has been opened out and the canal then crosses the deep Medlock valley at its narrowest point. Waterhouses aqueduct, about 40 ft above the river, is stone-built with a keyhole-shaped arch and sides curved to resist lateral pressure. Beyond this is the first lock, the chamber still good but the bottom gates lying below. Above is a wide triangular pound, and the canal makes a sixty-degree turn to the left and rises through a staircase of two locks, both filled in, and a single top lock to Waterhouses junction. Between the top lock and the staircase is a wide pound which would have had to provide two lockfuls of water while maintaining a reasonable level.

At the junction, the Fairbottom arm comes in from the right and

Waterhouses aqueduct on the Hollinwood arm over the Medlock

the main canal continues straight on towards Crime Lake. The towpath forms the south side of this lake along the top of an earth bank across a small valley. The lake itself, held by the bank, is a quarter of a mile long and provided water for lockage.

Crime bridge, under Cutler Hill Road, has now been filled up and the towpath beyond is in private ground. The canal without water runs in a curve through fields at Woodhouses, beneath Cutler Hill Road again and then begins to lose its identity. It is still traceable beyond Hollins Road and up to the Manchester Road at Hollins Wood, and the bridge parapets beside these two roads are still standing. Three locks used to counteract the slope of the ground but no trace of them remains today.

To return to Waterhouses junction, the towpath eastwards along the Fairbottom branch makes excellent walking for three-quarters of a mile, as far as the Oldham Road. The canal runs along the side of the Medlock valley near to the top and is reminiscent of the upper lengths of the Peak Forest canal. For most of the way it is in good order, but reeds and rushes fill its channel and there appears to have been slight subsidence at the eastern end. It is in water here and is fished by anglers.

The canal is filled in, fenced off and private beyond the Oldham Road. A mill stands across the way with the name THOMAS KERFOOT & CO. LTD. MANUFACTURING CHEMISTS, and on the tall chimney is the word VAPEX! The road bridge is supported by a large girder marked M.S. & L. RY. CO. A.C. DEPT. 1868.

The little area around the Waterhouses locks, the Fairbottom branch, and Crime Lake is well worth a visit both for the attractive setting and for the remains of what was once a busy coal canal. The same cannot be said of the Stockport branch, which ran through Gorton and Reddish into Stockport through a predominantly built-up area. Most of the canal has disappeared, though the bridges and their parapets help to mark out its almost straight line. Perhaps the most interesting point is in Stockport itself near the canal terminus. The roundabout at the northern end of Tiviot Way has removed the bridge before the terminus, but Wharf Street has the canal parapets, and the large bulk of the Albion Mills stands beside the wharf, which was once busy with boats carrying coal, grain and flour.

The Peak Forest canal links with the Ashton at the aqueduct over the Tame and runs practically south along the side of the deepening Tame Valley. The area is semi-derelict and is being restored to countryside by the Civic Trust for the North West. At first the canal is badly littered, for it runs beside the huge Dukinfield refuse dump and wind carries plastic bags and other lightweight material into it. Soon, however, the town of Hyde is reached, with its factories, one bearing the famous name of Adamson. Many of the stone buildings have the grace and proportions we associate with the early days of the nineteenth century. An old canal stable building is being restored by the Peak Forest Canal Society to be their headquarters.

Bridge 7 is an attractive turnover bridge carrying the towpath to the other side of the canal. Such bridges were so constructed that the horse could pass beneath before crossing over, and the rope would not then need to be unhitched. The open country starts from this point and extends for practically the whole of the remaining length of the canal. It is still on the side of the Tame Valley, curving around the bluffs in the hills and dominated for some distance by the huge, solitary Gee-X mill. The next village is Woodley, and here the canal dives into the first of its tunnels, only 176 yards long but very narrow, for nearly half its width is taken up by a towpath. Beyond the tunnel the canal lies mostly in a deep cutting with grassy banks crossed by a big wide railway bridge beneath which the voice echoes. The old council offices of Bredbury and Romiley are up the slope on the right and the town bridge carries the main road.

Outram's Marple aqueduct over the river Goyt

A second tunnel at Hyde Bank carries the canal through a watershed to the Goyt valley itself. The tunnel is wide and low, 308 yards long, and the towpath climbs up over the top. In bygone days the horse would be led by this route and the boatmen would place boards on either side of the fore end, hooked firmly on to the boat, and would walk the boat through the tunnel with their feet on the side walls. This method was known as legging, and the longer tunnels had professional leggers who did nothing else.

Beyond the tunnel the canal is mostly in deep woodlands which fall away to the river Goyt a hundred feet below and climb up to the top of a rocky hillside. There was once a third tunnel at Rose Hill, opened out early in the canal's history, but the narrow channel with its towpath still lies between rocky walls.

Next stands the most impressive structure on any of the canals in the area – the Marple aqueduct. The Goyt valley is deep, wooded and narrow, and the aqueduct crosses it in three great arches. On the towpath side there is a stone parapet, but the narrow channel is bounded on the farther side by a stone bank and a sheer drop of almost one hundred feet into the river! There is no path on this side and no need for boatmen to leave the safety of the craft, but the drop is certainly awe-inspiring. The whole effect is slightly lessened by the neighbouring railway viaduct, built about fifty years later. George Borrow saw the aqueduct and considered it to be a supreme work of man.

The canal climbs 208 ft up the wooded hillside through sixteen deep stone-built locks, and the banks and bridges are constructed of the same material. About half way up, a road crosses the flight, and beyond it a warehouse stands where Samuel Oldknow had his boats loaded under cover. Above the warehouse, the locks are close together and the grounds of the Marple council offices sweep down to the lockside. The main road from Marple's shopping centre crosses the canal on Posset Bridge and provides the best access for visitors. The bridge owes its name to Oldknow, who promised the workmen a posset of ale if they finished the bridge by a certain date. They did!

The pound below the bridge was restored by the Marple Civic Society and forms a pleasant little mooring for boats stopping for tea.

Oldknow's warehouse by Marple locks

There is a narrow oval tunnel carrying the towpath beneath the road for the horses to use and an even smaller passage with steps for boatmen to reach the lock. There used to be a branch to the left which swung round beneath the bridge to an interesting series of canal buildings adjoining the Marple limekilns. These were built into a vertical rock face, and an arm of the canal above the locks ran close to the top. Limestone and coal from pits close to the canalside were brought by boat to this arm and both were loaded into the kilns. The burnt lime was shovelled out at the bottom and loaded under cover into other boats on the Posset Bridge pound. The kilns themselves look not unlike a medieval ruin, and it is said that Samuel Oldknow, living on the opposite side of the valley, had them built with this in mind. The top locks stand close together by Lockside, with short pounds between. Long, sickle-shaped side-ponds run out from these to provide sufficient water to fill the very deep locks without dropping in level too much.

Once through Marple top lock we are in another world, for the upper pound of the Peak Forest canal is one of the highest lengths of navigable water in the entire country's canal system. A good towpath follows the whole six and a half miles as the canal curves round the flanks of the high hills. The Goyt valley lies below, used by railways and the A6 road as well as the navigation. Far off to the south-east, Kinderscout, the highest point in the Peak District, stands steep-sided but flat-topped against the sky. The valley is carved into the Millstone Grit, and the buildings and walls are of this rugged brown material. The house at the junction was once used by Jinks the boat builder, and this, the roving bridge opposite, the lime kilns and the ancient stone farmhouse up on the hill are all listed for preservation.

The navigation is a fine example of a contour canal, for once a suitable level was chosen by the surveyors the line followed the contour all along the hillside. It swings gently round the bluffs and bends sharply where the streams indent the hills. In earlier canals like the Caldon, near Stoke on Trent, such corners were really sharp, but they are eased on the Peak Forest by short embankments with the stream rushing beneath in a culvert. On occasions these places have proved to be points of weakness, for a blocked culvert can build up so great a volume of water that its sheer weight can cause a breach. Such a breach occurred at Disley in 1972 through abnormally heavy rain which made the canal overflow its banks. These gave way, and a 50 ft hole opened up and swallowed several moored boats.

Following the canal south from Marple, the towpath crosses to the east side at Brick Bridge and the hillside is so steep that the view is over the chimney pots of the houses. The well built stone wall which once bordered the towpath for nearly the whole of its length is broken and missing in several places, the stones either in the canal or lying down the slope of the steep hillside. Most of them could be salvaged, and it would be a splendid job for a civic society to rebuild the wall with the original materials.

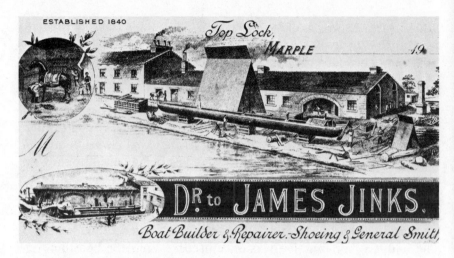

Jinks's boatyard by Marple top lock, from a bill heading

Jinks's house today, by Marple top lock

As on the Ashton and lower Peak Forest canals there are several swing bridges, some with a raised footbridge and some without. These must be opened for the passage of a boat and closed again afterwards. The last one before the terminus used to be particularly heavy but has now been replaced by a lift bridge. A lock windlass is needed to raise it, and it requires ninety-six turns. It is a very safe mechanism, however, for, being a worm drive, it cannot reverse of its own accord, flinging off the windlass and dropping the bridge too quickly.

South of Marple, Samuel Oldknow's village of Mellor lies across the valley, its church standing boldly on the hill top. Three miles along the canal is Disley, with a steep walk up from the mooring to reach the shops and the Ram's Head. It was at this historic inn that shareholders first met to decide to build the canal. A mile beyond is New Mills, or more correctly New Mills Newtown, for the old village is on the opposite side of the valley, now narrowed to a gorge. A boat hire firm has taken over some of the interesting stone buildings which were once served by the canal and has dredged out a small marina. Just beyond is a long, low, sloping building where rope used to be made, the great length being necessary for the lengths of rope to be twisted by a travelling carriage. In the valley itself are occasional mills, and a tall stone viaduct carries the railway lines across to the east side.

Beyond Furness Vale, through three bridges with the delightful names of Bongs, Greensdeep and Bothomes Hall, is the junction of the main canal with the Whaley Bridge arm. The main canal turns left to Bugsworth, or Buxworth as it has officially been called since 1931, and swings across the valley on an embankment and two aqueducts, the first for a farm track and the second for the river Goyt. It then enters the famous basins, disused for fifty years but now being restored by the Inland Waterways Protection Society.

These basins and the tramway which reached them were described by Peter Clowes[6] and by Brian Lamb in a manuscript for the Railway and Canal Historical Society. Some of Lamb's collection of photographs were to be seen at one time in the Navigation Inn at Bugsworth. The basins are well worth an extended visit, for they can be traced in detail.

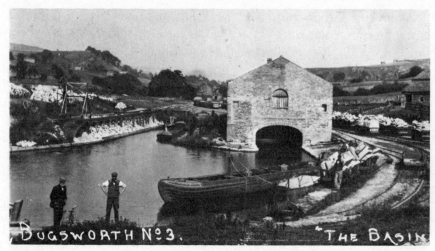

The top basin at Bugsworth, about 1912. Note the 'tippler' above the limestone quay

Bugsworth middle basin today. The Peak Forest tramway was on top and the limestone quay by the canalside

Following the towpath across the aqueduct, the canal curves gently round to the right past a mill and a row of cottages and then on to the gauging lock. This is a narrow, stone-built lock without gates but with grooves for stop planks, where boats could be gauged for weight of cargo by the depth to which they were loaded. Beside this is the stone-built wharfinger's house, which also contained his office. He was responsible for recording every load that went out.

The canal widened again into the entrance basin, which divided into two, the lower basin extending parallel to the road and the much larger middle basin swinging round to the right. The level of the road adjoining the lower basin climbs a few feet, and many of the stone blocks that carried the rails of the Peak Forest tramway are still in place. This was the site of the tippler, an apparatus which consisted of two huge wheels joined together, into which a truck could be pushed. A man climbing the spokes would tip the truck, one end of which was hinged. As this opened, the stone fell into the boats waiting below. The wider middle basin curved back to the road, with a short arm extending to the north. A number of limekilns lined its south bank and a small wharf reached by steps adjoined the road carrying the tramway. At this point the complex is crossed by a road from Chinley on which stands the Navigation Inn. Beyond the bridge is the extensive upper basin, with arms which used to run beneath warehouses. Early photographs show the wharfs on the north side with limestone piled upon them and a further tippler to load stone direct from the trucks into the waiting boats. The base of a wharfside crane can still be seen on the western side.

The tramway system was very extensive indeed. The main line went up the Blackbrook valley at a gentle slope, passed through the short Stodhart tunnel near Chapel Milton, reached Chapel Townend and climbed to the top of the hill on an inclined plane. The bottom of its five-hundred-yard length can be seen from the road from Chaple en le Frith to Buxton just beyond the fork to Hathersage. At the top of the plane, the old line can be followed very clearly running close to the Manchester to Buxton line and passing under the Buxton road to reach the famous quarries of Dove Holes.

Clowes gives a good description of the actual working of the tramway. The trucks were quite small, each holding about two and a half tons, and their unflanged wheels ran on a track of rails with an L-shaped section. These rails, 3 ft long, rested on cast iron chairs pegged into stone block sleepers. Horses would pull a train of trucks from the quarries to the first gentle slope, where the horses would be unhitched. The trucks then ran by gravity to the top of the incline, where not more than eight were hitched on to a long rope which passed round an 18 ft diameter wooden drum and down to the bottom of the incline. At the lower end, the rope was hitched on to empty trucks which the full ones would draw up as they descended. At the bottom, the trucks would be collected and linked up again and allowed to run gently down the hill through the tunnel and on to Bugsworth. A brakeman rode on the axle pin of the first truck and applied a primitive brake by thrusting an iron bar into the spokes and jamming the wheels, a method that led to many accidents. The empty trucks were drawn back from Bugsworth by teams of horses.

The other tramways led from gritstone quarries much nearer to the canal, and setts were transported to many towns in south Lancashire. All these tramways are good examples of the work of Benjamin Outram, who, besides being the canal engineer, was also a partner in the Butterley ironworks where the rails were made.

Bugsworth emphasises the close links between the canals and the early tramways and railways laid to bring stone or coal from neighbouring quarries and pits. So often the stone came from the hillside above the canal and gravity was the main motive force. The area is rich in such examples, and these include the Caldon Low tramway from the quarries to the Caldon canal and a host of others round the edge of the Peak District.

At Whaley Bridge a completely different type of railway was to be built, foreshadowing later developments. The half-mile arm of the canal to Whaley Bridge ends in a small triangular basin with an interesting stone building at the terminus. The channel passes under the centre of the building and ends a few feet beyond in an enclosed feeder from the reservoir at Todbrook. The building has wings on both sides, and a few years ago rails were visible running in from the back. This was the transshipment building from the railway to the canal where lime and other goods could be loaded from the train to the boat under cover. The railway was the Cromford and High Peak, permitted by Act of Parliament in 1825 and completed in 1831. The engineer was Josias Jessop, son of William Jessop, who built the Cromford canal and who, like Outram, was connected with the Butterley ironworks. The construction and working are well described by A. Rimmer.[37]

Richard Arkwright's Cromford was served by the Cromford canal, which was linked by the Erewash to the river Trent. Richard Arkwright and Samuel Oldknow were close friends and business associates, and a link between the two canals on either side of the Pennines had obvious advantages. The line was first surveyed for a canal, but the tremendous heights that it would have had to scale and the problems of feeding it with water militated against its construction. By 1825 the Stockton and Darlington railway had been opened and things were very different from the days when the Peak Forest tramway was built. A railway was clearly more logical. Though the first rails were 3 ft lengths of cast iron, they were designed for flanged wheels and were laid at Stephenson's standard gauge. The Act permitted waggons to be propelled by stationary or locomotive steam engines or other sufficient power. The railway age had begun.

8

The Manchester and Salford Junction Canal

If you walk down Oxford Street from St Peter's Square, you come to Great Bridgewater Street, running south from the right-hand side. The very name suggests canals, though it does not in fact link with the Bridgewater. Half-way down, however, where the street bends to the right, there is the stone balustrade of a bridge. Looking over the left-hand side, you can see the Rochdale canal running nearly parallel with the street, and a small branch runs under the bridge from a junction above lock 89. The branch, which has been filled in, runs northwards into a considerable area of land which has recently been cleared. The bridge is a typical Rochdale Canal structure, built around 1800, and the branch ran alongside wharves and warehouses which have now disappeared.

A few years ago the course of the canal was used for car parking and several warehouses were still to be seen backing on to it. The branch used to run about three hundred yards and turn sharply to the right to pass under Chepstow Street, though this length has been abandoned for many years and there are no signs beyond the street itself. Half-way along the main length, however, another branch ran towards Lower Mosley Street, which crossed it on a brick bridge. This bridge is of different design from that on Great Bridgewater Street and is clearly an example of what is often known as 'railway architecture'. It was built about 1840 and marks the beginning of the Manchester and Salford Junction canal, which used to run from this point north-westwards to the river Irwell half a mile away.

Tracing the line from this point, it would appear to have run beneath Central station, Watson Street, and the Great Northern Railway goods depot. It would have passed beneath Deansgate and Camp Street and the Granada television studios to enter the Mersey beyond Water Street. Sure enough, the junction is visible beyond Water Street, south of the Victoria and Albert warehouses and about a hundred and fifty yards up-river from the entrance of the Manchester, Bolton and Bury canal on the other side.

I had heard of the great tunnel beneath Deansgate and wondered how much of the canal might still be seen between Lower Mosley Street and Water Street. I therefore paid a visit to Central station, which was then fully operating, asked the stationmaster for permission to explore the huge underground car park, and at length was allowed to go and poke around. There was nothing to be seen, however, as this section of the canal had been completely obliterated when the station was built in 1875.

I then wrote to Granada Television. They said they would be delighted to show me their tunnel and fixed a date and time. I went, and was taken into a basement room where a locked door led on to a staircase down into the tunnel itself. We armed ourselves with torches and set out to explore.

My first impression was one of size and freshness, for the tunnel was dry, having been drained during the last war for use as an air raid shelter. It was stone-built, with a towpath along the north side, and appeared to be about seventeen feet high and twenty-five feet across. The Act of Parliament shows that it was constructed for boats, barges and flats, and the typical Mersey and Irwell craft were clearly envisaged. A series of cross-walls had been built during the war to contain blast, and I was told that there were about sixteen of these in the quarter-mile length of the tunnel. I was also told that goods used to be hoisted up into the railway depot in bygone days, but we were not able to get far enough along to see anything of the hoist.

The city's central reference library holds a series of large-scale Ordance Survey maps of Manchester printed in the 1840s, a few years after the canal was completed. Loss of water was the main problem, as there was no natural feeder except the Rochdale canal, which could not possibly have spared water from a short length between locks. A stop lock had in fact been built at the Lower Mosley Street end to safeguard the Rochdale's supplies. Beyond this, two pairs of locks were sited in the area where Central station was later to be built, and a pumping engine lifted water back to the top level. The canal then entered the tunnel west of Watson Street and continued beneath Deansgate and Camp Road to reappear just beyond Atherton Street. Another pair of locks dropped the level still further, and a single lock linked the navigation with the Irwell. Once more, a pump was required to lift water from the level of the Irwell to the top of the paired locks to replace what was used.

The history of this remarkable and very expensive canal, which was to lose much of its value even before it was completed, is recorded by Hadfield and Biddle.[15] The Manchester, Bolton and Bury joined the Irwell on its north side but there was no link with the canals in Manchester nearer than the Bridgewater locks at Runcorn. A navigable tunnel through from the river to the Rochdale had been suggested as early as 1801, and another four years later, but nothing came of either. Goods had to be off-loaded at the river company's wharfs and taken across Manchester by cart. When the Bill was sent to Parliament in 1836 the preamble emphasised the traffic problems in the centre of the town, and this ensured support from the townspeople and traders. Congestion was a problem even then.

The idea of a canal at this time was first raised at a meeting of the Mersey and Irwell shareholders, and it quickly caught on. The Bridgewater company, realising how much trade would be lost, suggested the alternative link with their canal to the Irwell at Hulme. As the two navigations were within a few yards of one another at this point, it was the obvious place to make contact. The Mersey and Irwell company were still wary of the Bridgewater and felt that it would be safer to have a separate link, so they went ahead with the promotion of their Bill. They ensured support from the Bridgewater company by a clause allowing that company to build their own Hulme locks, which were completed in 1838, a year before the Manchester and Salford Junction canal was opened. A further clause ensured that the level of the water above the stop lock should be 6 in.

above that of the Rochdale canal to safeguard the latter's water supply.

As was only to be expected, with the easy alternative route, the junction canal did not attract the estimated trade. It also had troubles with its pumping engines, its stop lock and one of the lock walls, and a further Act was necessary to find more money. Half this money came from the river navigation or its shareholders, who were soon induced to take over the junction canal and its debts and liabilities. Though maintenance cost considerably more than revenues from tolls, it added wharfs and basins to the Irwell and brought in additional traffic. Furthermore, because of this link with the Rochdale and the Ashton, there is little doubt that the Mersey and Irwell was a much more valuable acquisition when it was bought by Lord Francis Egerton for the Bridgewater trustees a few years later.

Once the junction canal had become the property of the Bridgewater trustees it lost its value as a competitive route. When the Cheshire Lines railway decided on their Manchester terminus at Central station in 1872, they first planned to build it over the canal. Three years later they obtained a second Act which allowed them to fill in the section between Lower Mosley Street and Watson Street, and the canal, as a junction, ceased.

The western end, adjoining the Irwell, continued as a useful series of docks. When the Great Northern Railway goods depot was built in 1899 over the tunnel, this formed a valuable interchange, last used regularly in 1922 and abandoned in 1936. The eastern end had been obliterated, but the basins adjoining the Rochdale were not filled in until after the last war. Soon, however, they too will be beneath modern buildings and the only traces of the expensive and little used junction canal will be the exit to the Irwell, the link with the Rochdale above lock 89 and the three bridges between.

9

The Compstall Navigation

The Compstall navigation was a very small private canal, entirely independent of and unconnected to the waterway system of the country. It is included here because it is local, and quite different from all other canals described. Most canals have required an Act of Parliament, to safeguard owners of the land through which they were to pass. This was unnecessary when all the land where the canal was to be dug belonged to a single landowner, provided that it had no effect on his neighbours. It must not, for instance, divert water from someone else's streams or upset the drainage pattern of a wider area. Like some of the agricultural canals of south-west England, such as the Torrington, the little Compstall navigation was an example of a waterway restricted to the land of one owner, and like them it developed in its own special way.

The village of Compstall lies between Hyde and Marple in the beautiful Etherow valley and is most easily reached by road from Romiley or Marple Bridge. It owes as much to one family, the Andrews, as Mellor did to Samuel Oldknow. According to R. E. Thelwall,[42] Thomas Andrew was printing cotton textiles in Harpurhey before the end of the eighteenth century. He was a man of means, and his two sons, George and Thomas, had moved to Compstall and started dyeing and printing by 1820. Four years later they were also spinning and weaving cloth, dyeing and printing it themselves and selling it. The work at first appears to have been carried out in farm buildings, the weaving by hand looms in cottages.

As the business grew they built dwellings for the workmen, a Methodist church, a school and then St Paul's Anglican church, and constructed a bridge over the Etherow to replace the ford.

The value of the Etherow to provide water power was obvious and was clearly one of the reasons for choosing Compstall, but there does not appear to be a record of the construction of the great weir. Certainly by 1839, when the 'Lily' wheel, said to have been the largest waterwheel of its type in the country, was built by Fairbairn and Lilley, the weir and leat were already in being. There are said to have been two wheels before this, and it would appear that the water power was harnessed early on.

The weir was constructed three-quarters of a mile up river from Compstall bridge and the site of the mill, and a canal-sized leat was built alongside the river. This widened out into a reservoir of several acres' extent by the mill and provided a great volume of water to drive the wheel. In addition, the damming of the river produced a lake above the weir, connected to the leat by a large sluice whose gear still stands in a small building near the river. A mud trap which had to be emptied regularly was built within the sluice, which was opened each morning and closed again at night. Mr Hurst, warden of the Country Park, has told me that so much water was used to drive the great wheel that the river was often emptied both above and below the weir by evening! This was probably partly due to the reduced flow in the river which occurred after Manchester built the Woodhead reservoirs.

The thirty-foot-high weir is sickle-shaped and stepped, and is one of the largest in the country. Originally built of bricks, it has had to be repaired from time to time with concrete. Slots had originally been made to set boards along the top to raise the water level even higher.

The leat runs between the river and the woodland and is wide, deep and stone-sided. It has sluices at intervals to return any excess of water to the river. Up to this point it was typical of many channels built to bring a head of water to drive a mill. It also came to be used as a navigation, and this may have been one of the reasons for its size and superior construction. The Etherow valley at Compstall cuts deeply into coal measures, and small mines were opened up in the wooded hills. Mr Hurst told me that the villagers used to climb down into the river channel in the evenings when the flow had stopped and dig coal out of the bed! Light tramways on wooden rails appear to have been laid to carry the coal to the canal, though nothing is visible of these today. We know that the leat was used as a navigation, for special tub boats were constructed and two of them are still visible.

These boats are of extremely interesting design. They are 22 ft long, 6 ft 5 in. wide and 3 ft deep, and rectangular in plan, with steeply sloping, punt-like ends and vertical sides. They are constructed of cast iron plates riveted together and strengthened with knees where the sides join the bottom. Around the top edge is two-inch angle iron with towing rings affixed and short lengths of hand-made chain. One very unusual feature is a horseshoe-shaped rowlock sunk in a slot approximately four feet from one end, and three similar slots occur on the other side and at the other end. It seems most likely that this was used with an oar or a paddle for steering. Such a boat, loaded to within perhaps six inches of the waterline, could hold about eight tons of coal.

The one boat was carefully excavated by a group of local Scouts, and stands close to the water at the head of the navigation. The metal is very thin in places, and a number of holes occur which would, no doubt, in the past have been patched up by a blacksmith. Such a patch already occurs at one end. During its working life the boat would have been horse-drawn, the horse on one or other side of the canal, either of which was suitable as a towpath. Perhaps a horse would have drawn a string of such boats, linked together by their towing rings and steered by a man sitting on the load, using the rowlock of the last boat.

The other is still largely beneath the ground in the woodlands by the riverside above the head of the navigation. Its edge is visible and it is clearly of the same dimensions and of similar construction to the one excavated. It would appear to have been run up on to the bank at some time when perhaps the river was high, and gradually sank into the alluvial mud. The fact that it was on the riverside and not beside the canal suggests that it was used on the river, at least at the time when it was beached. Mr Hurst knew of no coal pits farther up the valley, and the boat may have been used for maintenance and for clearing floating rubbish, which would otherwise block the channel or damage the weir. When empty, or loaded with logs and brushwood, the boat would be of shallow draft and may have been rowed across the wide, shallow stretches of the river.

Before the end of the nineteenth century the firm of George Andrew and Co. amalgamated with Calico Printers Association. Since that date, first the printing section was closed in 1901, then the spinning in 1926 and finally the whole mill in 1966. Some of the buildings have disappeared and the rest are occupied by a number of firms.

Before the 1974 changes in local government administration, the forward-looking council of Bredbury and Romiley bought a large piece of the Etherow valley, including the canal, and established a country park, maintaining it in its natural state. It is thus possible today to park a car near the mill or reach the village by bus and walk the length of the canal past the boat to the weir and beyond. A nature trail has been laid out through the woodlands and along the canalside and a small guide notes the animal and plant life to be seen. The whole area is one of great beauty and of considerable interest, not least to the waterways enthusiast, and the cottage-lined streets of the old village are still named after members of the Andrew family.

10

The Manchester Ship Canal

The Manchester Ship Canal differs from all other navigations in the area in being a great ocean seaway linking the docks of Manchester with ports in all parts of the world. There are close links with Canada, and specially designed ships penetrate the canals to reach ports on the Great Lakes.

Apart from size, there is a real difference between ship canals and barge canals, for barges are low and the restricted headroom allows road and rail bridges to cross at minimum height. Ships, on the other hand, with their tall masts and high superstructure require so much greater headroom that bridges must either be carried high above them or be capable of swinging to allow a clear passage. In Holland, Belgium and other countries where large ships come far inland, some roads are taken beneath the navigation in tunnels. One other ship canal was built in England as early as 1824, from Sharpness to Gloucester, to bring ships up to the Gloucester docks. All the bridges along the sixteen-mile route, including a major railway bridge, were made to swing or lift.

The idea of a ship canal to Manchester was considered on a number of occasions. Ships sailed on the Mersey and Irwell, but they were small coasters, and the Bridgewater canal was restricted to barges. Sea-going vessels had to off-load their goods in Liverpool or at one of the other Mersey ports to be transferred on to the small vessels of the inland navigations. The original charter of the Port of Liverpool defined its extent from the Dee to Warrington, and Liverpool could therefore charge dues on any transshipment in the Mersey whether or not her own docks were used. Throughout most of the nineteenth century the Liverpool dues were said to be exorbitant and oppressive. Leech[24] quotes an example of the dues taken in 1852–53, amounting to £115,000 clear of expenses, of which only £4,770 was spent on improving the port and river. Of the rest, money was used to reduce the town's rates, and £3,000 was even spent on the library, museum and observatory!

The first serious attempt to build a ship canal was in 1824, when Matthew Hedley formed a company to raise £1 million and William Chapman surveyed the route. It was decided to avoid Liverpool completely so as to be clear of any possible port dues and to start from the river Dee at Dawpool, near Heswall. There was to have been a tidal basin, a half-tide lock and a dock at high-tide level, 1,000 ft long and 300 ft wide. From this the canal was to run along the riverside, cross the Wirral by the Backford gap, used already by the Shropshire Union canal, swing eastwards to cross the Trent and Mersey at Preston Brook and follow the line of the Bridgewater through Lymm and Altrincham to south Manchester. It was to be designed to carry ships of 400 tons, and it is worth remembering that few early nineteenth-century merchant sailing vessels were larger than this. A Bill was sent to Parliament but was thrown out because the levels had not been properly shown. It is fortunate that the canal was never built, for even if it had been enlarged the Dee would have been harder to keep clear of silt.

Sir John Rennie was asked by the Mersey and Irwell company to report on possible improvements to their navigation, and he carried out a survey between Bank Quay, Warrington, and Runcorn in 1838. He considered that it could be deepened and that a ship canal could be extended up to Manchester. Two years later H. R. Palmer and J. F. Bateman were requested to advise the company. Palmer suggested a twelve-foot-deep canal to Manchester with a series of new cuts and a reduction of locks to six, to take ships of 400-600 tons. Similar improvements were to take place on the Weaver, where locks were reduced from eleven to four and 500 ton craft were accommodated. Bateman favoured a barrier from Runcorn to Widnes across the narrowest part of the estuary, with flood gates and a lock, giving deep water to Warrington. Neither of these schemes was implemented, though the rivers were deepened two years later to take larger craft. After this the navigation was bought by the Bridgewater trustees and no further plans were envisaged.

In 1876 George Hicks decided that something must be done. The old navigation was in a very poor state, and Manchester and the neighbouring towns were in desperate need of better communications. Because of the absurdly high dues in the port of Liverpool, it was said to be cheaper to bring goods to Hull and transport them across England by railway, but even the railway charges were too high for the Lancashire traders. Hicks wrote a letter to the *Manchester Guardian* which caught the eye of Hamilton Fulton, an engineer experienced in the improvement of navigations who had already worked on the river Nene, and Fulton replied. Hicks obtained the interest of the Chamber of Commerce, asked both Fulton and Boyd Dawkins, the Manchester University geologist, to prepare reports, and a model was made and exhibited.

A great deal of lobbying was necessary, and in 1881 Sir William Harcourt drew a comparison with Glasgow, where the river had been dredged to the city, adding, 'Heaven helps those who help themselves.' Further correspondence appeared in the papers and pamphlets were written, extolling the virtues or emphasising the difficulties of a major ship canal to Manchester. Clearly a leader of real force was necessary, and such a leader was found in Daniel Adamson. Adamson was a north-country engineer and industrialist who had settled in Manchester and had built up a large business in Hyde. In June 1882 he summoned a meeting in his house, 'The Towers' (now the home of the Shirley Institute), at which the mayor, chief citizens and industrialists attended. He drew attention to the improvements for shipping on the Tyne, Tees and Clyde. He stressed that if the Suez canal could be built in an uninhabited desert a comparable undertaking must be possible in the valleys of the Mersey and Irwell. Fulton then outlined his plans for a ship canal and Hicks spoke of its probable effects on trade and revenue. As a result of the meeting Fulton and E. Leader Williams, engineer to the second

Bridgewater and the first Weaver navigations, were asked to work together to produce a costed scheme. When they came to discuss their plans the two engineers differed radically, and each was therefore asked to concentrate on his own separate scheme for consideration in September. J. Abernethy, a consulting engineer, was invited to comment on the rival schemes.

It is worth considering the two plans to see how they differed. Fulton proposed a tidal ship canal at sea level the whole way. He pointed out that the river had a natural course of fifty miles and the present navigation had shortened it to forty-two. He proposed that the tidal portion should be straightened and dredged to a depth of 22 ft below low water. A nearly straight channel should be excavated to this same depth, with passing places every three or four miles. He calculated that this would bring a tidal range in Manchester of about fifteen feet, and the great body of water sweeping in and out would help to keep the channel clear and would also clear the bar. He proposed a basin in Manchester with a fall from ground level to the quay wall, and pointed out that bridges would need to be raised only a little with the canal so far beneath. He pointed out that both the Suez and the proposed Panama canals ran in deeper cuttings along their courses. At that time most vessels calling at Liverpool were less than 3,500 tons and could use such a navigation at all states of the tide. The Bridgewater canal would be 65 ft above such a canal: a trough could be designed to raise it a few feet higher, and this could also be done for the railways or swing bridges provided. His estimate of the total cost was £5,072,921. He was prepared to design two locks above Barton aqueduct, each with a lift of 15 ft, if they were considered desirable.

Leader Williams planned a canal with locks. Once more, he proposed to use the tidal river as far as Latchford, near Warrington, dredging the tidal portion to a depth of 22 ft below low water and using retaining walls. He pointed out that the present navigation had a fall of about sixty feet between Manchester and Warrington and that four locks could raise the ship canal by this amount. He emphasised that the deeply dredged channels of the Tyne and Clyde were mud-filled, while the Irwell flowed over rock. Cutting so deep a channel would therefore be more expensive than building locks.

Furthermore the docks in Manchester would need to be excavated to a depth of 92 ft and quays would be inconvenient so far below the ground. He would use flood sluices as on the Weaver and provide high or swing bridges for the railways and roads. He proposed a swing aqueduct for the Bridgewater canal and drew attention to the Anderton boat lift, which coped successfully with similar problems of retaining water while the caissons moved. His estimate of cost was £5,160,000, and he believed he could complete the work in four years.

Both schemes were submitted to James Abernethy, who approved of Leader Williams's proposals, felt that the tidal channel ought to be dredged to a depth of 24 ft and estimated a total sum of £5,400,000. With regard to the tidal canal, he did not believe that the parallel sides would result in such a tidal range and felt that there could be problems of silting. He could not comment on the cost, as no detailed breakdown was contained in the Fulton report. The committee came out in favour of Leader Williams's scheme.

Having passed this hurdle, the canal supporters flung themselves into action. A committee was formed to have a Bill drafted and sent to Parliament, and Leech and others set about canvassing for a fund of £100,000 to cover the parliamentary expenses. Opposition quickly materialised, particularly from Liverpool and the railway companies, for both expected loss of revenue if the canal was ever completed. The Bridgewater canal owners revived the scheme of extending the canal from Runcorn to Widnes and on to Liverpool, and there was even a suggestion of a Lancashire plateway with traction engines hauling trucks from one town to the other.

By November parliamentary notices had been issued and plans and sections deposited. In January 1883 came the first blow, when opponents were able to point out that the Standing Orders had not been complied with. Petitions were received from the Mersey Docks Board and, in addition, the London and North Western Railway which drew attention to the fact that the promoters had neglected to provide plans and sections of the Mersey low-water channel. The promoters retorted that this was impossible, as the channel shifted about the estuary. Because of this the Bill was not acceptable to the parliamentary examiners and an appeal had to be made direct to

Parliament. This all took up time, particularly as only six of the possible Lords committee turned up and the appeal had to be delayed to a more suitable date. However, Standing Orders were set aside and the Bill was allowed to go to Parliament on the condition that the creation of a tidal channel from Eastham to Runcorn was deleted and the promoters were prepared to make arrangements for this with the Mersey Docks Board.

The Bill was discussed and passed by the House of Commons and was sent to the House of Lords. Because of the early delay the season was now late; the Lords felt that the Bill was incomplete, and there was insufficient time to amend it before the close of the session. They declared on 4 August that it was 'not expedient to proceed this Session in Parliament'. Leech includes in his book Boddington's plan of the proposed canal as it was considered in the 1883 Bill with its entrance just short of the Old Quay at Runcorn. There were three locks side by side, with tidal gates and sluices at Walton, near Warrington, and locks at Irlam and Barton. Two railways at Warrington were to be carried beneath the canal in tunnels, and sailing ships and masted steamers were drawn using the navigation. There is even a suggested cut from Ellesmere Port across the Wirral to the Dee, though this was probably put in to show that the Mersey estuary was not of vital importance to the whole scheme. The estimated cost of the canal was given as £5,633,951.

The loss of the first Bill only spurred on the proposers, who set to work immediately to put right the faults and prepare for a further attempt. They were not going to fall into the same trap over Standing Orders and they thought that there would be little difficulty in producing a satisfactory Bill to carry through both Houses. This was deposited in November 1883 and came first before the Lords early in 1884. The plan differed from the previous one, showing locks at Barton, Irlam, Latchford and Runcorn, and the estimated cost was now £6,904,187. Once more there was opposition at every stage from Liverpool, the Mersey Docks Board and the railway companies, and the Bill was given a most thorough inspection by the committee of the House of Lords. It is said that at a crucial point their lordships looked out of their windows and saw a ship of about one thousand tons going down-river. As it reached Westminster Bridge it lowered both masts and funnel and slipped quietly beneath. This seemed to convince waverers, and they passed the Bill with the provisio that no work should start until £5 million had been subscribed. They were anxious that it should be in the hands of genuine industrialists and not speculators. There was great rejoicing in Manchester, for it was now felt that the main hurdle was safely passed. The Bill went on to the House of Commons.

At this point the opposition mounted their major attack. The Bill was read twice and referred to a strong committee, but there was still a time factor, and the opposition realised that it was possible to talk the Bill out. The promoters had to keep their evidence to a minimum, and this may have strengthened their case, as so much had been heard before. In June the Dock Board chairman said that if the promotors would drop the estuary work they would withhold their opposition. Yet on 1 August the Commons decided to throw the Bill out. Manchester was horrified.

So much money had been spent already and so much was at stake that a third Bill was deposited the following November. Leader Williams was asked to examine both sides of the estuary, for deep water reached as far south as Garston on the east and Eastham on the west. He and all the promotors considered that the Cheshire side was the more suitable, even though the Weaver and Shropshire Union canal both joined the estuary on that side. Another change of plan was to site the docks in the Pomona Gardens, which were in Manchester, rather than the racecourse, which was in Salford. Later this was to become the site of the largest dock.

The locks were to be at Mode Wheel, Barton, Irlam and Latchford, with a sea lock at Eastham which could be open for a short period around high water. Thus the spring tides would reach as far as Latchford and the long section around the Cheshire shore would show slight variations in level. The canal was therefore to be nearly twice as long as it had been first planned, with five sets of locks and sluices instead of the three in the first Bill and the four in the second. The scouring of the estuary and the building of the retaining walls were not now necessary, but much costly excavation of rock was envisaged in the area round Ince. On the other hand, some of the rock proved to be good building stone, and clay in other sections was used for brick-making. The estimated cost was £6,311,137 and the Bill asked for permission to raise £8 million.

Despite their offer to withdraw opposition the previous year, the Mersey Docks Board opposed the third Bill, which had a much easier time in the house of Lords. Their lordships had heard enough already and passed the Bill subject to the raising of £5 million within two years of royal assent, this sum in addition to the cost of purchasing the Bridgewater and the Mersey and Irwell. It will be recalled that the Bridgewater trustees had acquired the Mersey and Irwell some forty years earlier, and the whole concern had to be bought out even though the two rivers were all that were needed of the line of the ship canal.

This time the Bill passed quickly through the Commons and received the royal assent on 6 August 1885. There was great jubilation in and around Manchester, even though the three Bills had cost the promoters £172,500 and no doubt the opposition a similar sum.

Looking back now, it seems that the opposition was a good thing, for it meant that every aspect of the canal had had to be considered in the minutest detail. It is certainly doubtful whether the dredged channel with its retaining walls would have proved a success with so great a tidal range. Within a few years of the opening the whole canal was deepened from 26 ft to 28 ft and the tidal portion to a greater depth still. This might have been difficult with the earlier schemes, particularly with the plan proposed in the first Bill when railways were to tunnel beneath the canal.

Having finally succeeded with their Bill in Parliament, the promoters had to settle down and find the money. Daniel Adamson was convinced that this would not be difficult, for he thought that the working men of Manchester and district would come in their tens of thousands to put small savings into shares. His own workpeople were prepared to do two hours' overtime a week and put the money into a fund to buy shares, and he proposed shilling coupons like present-day savings stamps which would be convertible into shares. If £2 million could be collected in this manner, it was proposed that Rothschild's should be asked to raise the other £6 million. So small a commission was offered that it proved impossible to get the shares underwritten. Time went on, and in 1887, with only six months to go to raise the £5 million necessary to start, there was still no sign of the money coming in. Daniel Adamson, despite his great drive, had not the necessary financial experience, and a change was called for. The board of directors had to be strengthened and the chairman had to stand down. This Adamson did on 1 February with the words, 'I now retire most respectfully from the Board. I wish the canal every success and I hope the capital will soon be got. I know it will be if the matter is properly pursued and there will be nobody who will rejoice more than I shall when you at last get to work.'

Lord Egerton was nominated chairman and the money began to roll in. By 14 May £3 million of shares had been taken up, and a Bill was quickly put through Parliament to permit the issue of £4 million of preference shares. These were taken up by the two great merchant banks of Rothschild's and Baring's, and on 4 July the Bridgewater canal and the two rivers were purchased for £1,710,000 and paid for

Eastham locks under construction. Note the steam crane

by a single cheque, the largest that had ever been written! With the money in hand just in time, a start could be made.

It is worth considering for a moment the personality of Daniel Adamson, who was born in Durham in 1829 of poor parents and settled in Hyde to build up a firm making steel boilers. There is little doubt that the canal would never have been started had he not been at the helm. Contemporary portraits show him to have been a man of great presence and vitality, a man who would drive his colleagues to the utmost and himself even further. Having decided to take up the canal, he would brook no opposition, and failures made him all the more determined to succeed. As was only to be expected, a man with such force of character had faults as well as virtues. He was impatient and did not suffer fools gladly, and in giving evidence to Parliament both he and his claims seemed a bit larger than life. Eventually the raising of the money defeated him and he had to step down, but by that time he had built up a team which proved capable of dealing with the great and unforeseen difficulties which lay ahead.

Eastham locks and sluices just completed, about 1890

On 11 November 1887 Lord Egerton, accompanied by the rest of the directors, slipped quietly across to Eastham and cut the first sod. Leader Williams wheeled it away in a barrow, and the work had begun.

The contractor was Thomas Andrew Walker, a man of sixty, with very wide experience. He had worked in the construction of London underground railways and had built the famous Severn tunnel, a prodigious job at a time when little was known of the deep channels beneath the main river estuaries. The work was soon going ahead in all sections, and a total of sixteen thousand men were employed. In addition to the ninety-seven steam excavators and grabs a vast amount of work was done by men with spades and barrows. The description of horse barrow roads emphasises the actual human labour involved. Planks were laid up the steeply sloping sides of the canal as it was dug and horse gins were set up at the top. These consisted of drums mounted on vertical poles, with horizontal cross-pieces on to which the horse was harnessed. A rope was attached to the drum or to a horizontal shaft geared to the vertical spindle, and the other end ran down the slope. The barrow was coupled to this and drawn up the bank on the planks while the barrowman held the shafts and steered. If anything went wrong the barrow would crash back with its contents on to the unbalanced steerer, but a hundred barrow loads were pulled up each hour by this means. Coming down, the man went first, holding the barrow and sliding down the planks.

For the first two years all went well and the work proceeded apace. Then, in November 1889, Walker died, and his executors carried on the contracting. This was to prove a tragedy, for many things were to go wrong and Walker's cool competence was sorely missed.

During that year the Weaver and Randles sluices were built to carry surplus water from the rivers into the estuary, and the Gowy siphon was completed. The Gowy is only a minor river but it drains a considerable area of mid-Cheshire and carries a large volume of silt and sand in times of flood. The siphon carried the river beneath the canal and allowed it to discharge directly into the estuary. The huge lock gates were also under construction and were built of greenheart wood, so dense and resistant that it is actually heavier than water. A pair of lower gates for the main locks weighed 540 tons. The most important visitors during the year included the Shah of Persia and Mr Gladstone.

Late in 1889 the weather worsened, and an October gale on top of the high tide washed over the embankment at Ince, damaging the railway laid along the embankment. Worse was to follow, for in the November of the following year torrential rains occurred on both the 7th and the 24th and the rivers swept down in full flood. The waters overtopped the embankment in the upper reaches and carried away dams constructed to keep them out of the excavations. The whole canal from Latchford to the docks above Trafford Park was under forty feet of water. Photographs taken at the time show this huge sheet of swirling water, but even they are not so discouraging as those taken three weeks later when the giant pumps had cleared the excavations. The whole course was littered with piles of broken, upended waggons, together with machinery and debris of all kinds. Even this disaster did not complete the ravages of the elements, for the early weeks of 1891 were gripped by an unprecedented frost. This was followed by a freak thaw at the end of January which brought further floods to the area around Thelwall. There were yet other floods which broke into the workings in December 1891 and again in December 1892.

The total effect of these catastrophes was very serious indeed. Conditions were bad, and the men struck for higher wages. The contractors had great difficulties in solving the problems, and the huge extra costs of repair work swallowed up all the funds subscribed without producing the necessary results. At this point the local authorities stepped in, and in 1891 Manchester Corporation obtained an Act permitting them to put £3 million into the project. Salford too was prepared to raise £1 million and sent a Bill to Parliament to obtain the necessary powers but withdrew it as the money was not required. Oldham was also prepared to help financially if necessary, and the whole area was determined that the work should be completed successfully. Manchester very properly demanded directorships to oversee the spending of the money and in 1893 raised its commitment to £5 million.

By now there was an even greater determination to complete the canal whatever obstacles had to be cleared first. In June 1891 water was let into the canal between Eastham and Ellesmere Port, though the port itself was still connected to the estuary by a gap left intentionally in the embankment. In July it was determined to close this gap, and twenty-four hours only were set aside for the work, to minimise the hold-up of shipping in the busy port. On Saturday 11 July all was ready, with trucks on each side full of rocks and clay to tip into the gap. The work was to start at low tide and to continue as fast as possible to keep the rising tide out. All went well at first, but at two o'clock on Sunday morning the tide broke through and carried away the whole barrier. Reserve supplies of rock and clay kept for such an emergency were brought up, and at low tide the work was started afresh. Once more the dawn tide on Monday broke through. With

Saltport, where the Manchester Ship Canal is joined by the Weaver navigation, about 1895

shipping now building up both inside and outside the port, a third attempt was made, and the engineers watched with bated breath. This time the barrier held, and, as the tide dropped on the Tuesday, it was raised and strengthened. It has held ever since. Ellesmere Port was now linked to the estuary by the canal and ships had no more need of the little dockside lighthouse to guide them home.

Two months later, water was let into the Ince section and the Weaver was linked to Eastham by the canal. Saltport was established at the mouth of the river and ships carried salt from there to many parts of the world.

Despite the many problems the work continued, and in November 1893 the actual filling of the last section began. On 7 December a party of people went aboard the Mersey ferry *Snowdrop* at Liverpool landing stage and set off at 7.30 in the morning. By eight o'clock they had reached Eastham and were through the lock in ten and a half minutes. They reached Runcorn at 9.20 and continued to Latchford locks, which were negotiated in eight minutes. Irlam locks took twelve minutes and those at Barton seventeen, and they berthed at Pomona docks on time at three o'clock. Manchester was now an ocean port. It was open to traffic on 1 January 1894, and Queen Victoria herself performed an official opening ceremony on 21 May.

It was not until the final stages that Liverpool became really worried, for it had never expected the canal to be completed. There was talk of building cotton mills in Liverpool, and a shipping ring was formed to boycott the use of the canal altogether. The company obtained a further Act in 1904 to allow them to deepen the canal from 26 ft to 28 ft, and a great new dock was built on the site of the racecourse the following year. The huge industrial estate of Trafford Park came into being, with special low rates to attract a variety of industries from different parts of the country. A new shipping company, Manchester Liners, was established to develop North American traffic. Despite the success of these ventures trade was not drawn to the canal in the volume its promoters had hoped. Fierce opposition from the railway companies, shipping conferences and the port of Liverpool made the early years difficult until the first world war upset the established patterns of shipping. Not until 1950 did traffic reach the volume forecast for the seventh year of operation. The indirect benefits were probably more important, since the building of the canal and the industrialisation of Trafford Park stimulated the economic life of the city and its hinterland, increasing Manchester's importance as a centre for communications, for imports, and as the metropolitan centre of the North-west.[12] Today modern ships of around ten thousand tons bring trade from all parts of the world, and the port is particularly suited to the container system. Moreover the port of Manchester extends the whole way down the canal to the Queen Elizabeth oil dock at Eastham, opened in 1954 and capable of taking four large tankers at the same time.

Amongst the great engineering achievements in the construction of the canal the most notable is the swing aqueduct at Barton. It will be recalled that the Bridgewater canal crossed the old Irwell navigation on a three-arched stone aqueduct which gave sufficient headroom for barges and flats on the river below. The Ship Canal needed at least 70 ft of headroom, and it was therefore necessary to replace Brindley's masterpiece with a different type of structure which would allow large ships to pass. Leader Williams's swing aqueduct, built on the same principle as the many road bridges, was the solution accepted. This posed more problems than the latter, for the movable section was much heavier if water was to be allowed to stay in it and there was the further necessity of preventing leakage. The ends of both the tank and the canal had to be made watertight, and this was done by partitions similar to lock gates, which could be closed or opened back to the sides of the tank and the canal. Had the tank fitted tightly against the canal at both ends it could never have been swung. Had the necessary gap been left, the water would have poured through it. To make it leakproof, the narrow gap, which is slightly oblique, is closed by a rubber-shod iron wedge weighing twelve tons, the same section as the tank. When the tank is to be swung, the gates are closed and the wedge is moved by hydraulic rams; these allow a small quantity of water to escape and provide room for the tank to swing. When swung back, the wedges are replaced at both ends and they make a watertight seal before the gates are opened.

The tank is pivoted on sixty-four cast iron rollers, tapering inwards,

Horse boats on Barton swing aqueduct, about 1900

Barton aqueduct today

CTM-I

which run in a circular channel 25 ft across. In the centre of the pivot is a hydraulic press which has a total pressure of 900 tons. When operated, this takes more than half the total weight of the tank and water, and allows it to swing with less friction on the rollers. The tank itself is 235 ft long, 18 ft wide and 7 ft deep and is filled with water to a depth of 6 ft. There is a towpath 9 ft above water level, and the entire moving structure weighs 1,450 tons, including 800 tons of water.

The aqueduct is worth a close inspection, and the best way to do this is to come by boat on the Bridgewater canal, but it is also worth seeing from the land. It is, of course, private property, and permission to go up on to the small bridge on the south side or on to the towpath of the Bridgewater canal should be obtained from the Manchester Ship Canal Company. It may even be possible to time a visit to correspond with the passage of one of the large ships which tower above the onlooker. Today there is little apart from pleasure traffic on the Bridgewater, but the aqueduct is swung for their passage as well.

The easiest locks to reach by road are those at Latchford. A straight east-and-west road runs along the south side of the Ship Canal past the locks, and shipping can be watched at leisure. Here, and at Irlam, Barton and Mode Wheel, there are two locks side by side, the larger 600 ft long and 65 ft wide on the north and the smaller 350 ft long and 45 ft wide. Latchford has a rise of 12 ft 6 in. and the other three slightly more. When large ships use the canal they are normally accompanied by tugs which can come up in the smaller lock and be ready to take on the ship when it has risen in the larger.

At Eastham there are three locks side by side, 600 ft by 80 ft, 350 ft by 50 ft and 150 ft by 30 ft, and these are opened at both ends when the tide rises above a certain height. Eastham has storm gates opening outwards towards the estuary as a protection against rough weather during high tides.

Alongside each group of locks are the sluices which take the place of weirs. There are four at Mode Wheel and Barton, five at Irlam and three only at Latchford. Below Latchford, where the canal is partly tidal, two sluices have been built on the north side at Randles, east of Runcorn, and ten more opposite the mouth of the Weaver. These are gates, 30 ft wide, which can be raised to allow flood waters to escape.

At Eastham there are two only, rather smaller than the rest, for the locks themselves can deal with most of the flood waters which have not been passed into the estuary higher up. Thus the rivers and the canal are now controlled so completely that there can never be a repetition of the terrible floods which occurred during construction.

Because of the necessary headroom for ships, all bridges have had to be built high above the water with long approaches or have had to be made to swing. The high bridges include the two motorways M6 and M63 and a number of railways whose approaches are even longer, as their slopes have had to be more gentle. These are what are known as deviation bridges. When the railway companies received their Acts of Parliament, clauses stated that low-level bridges would have to be made movable if the Mersey and Irwell navigation was ever improved to accommodate larger vessels. By the end of the century, when the Ship Canal was built, traffic on the railways had expanded so much that movable bridges were out of the question and the high-level deviation bridges were built in their place. As the level of the canal below Latchford is affected by high tides, there are markers in the water indicating headroom. These are boards similar to those indicating depth of water, marked in numbers of feet which become less as the water rises.

The canal structures have been described in a number of publications. One of the most complete descriptions occurs in the magazine *Engineering* of 26 January 1894,[28] though the author remains anonymous. Leader Williams himself also gave an account.[50] In addition to the aqueduct, the locks, the bridges and sluices, the magazine account described fully some of the engineering equipment used in the excavation and construction.

The best way to see the canal today is by steamer trip between Manchester and Liverpool. These are organised regularly during the summer weekends by the Co-operative Travel Agency, using one of the old Mersey ferry steamers. A plan of the canal is available, and a commentary draws attention to the various works and places of interest *en route*. The ship, often the *Royal Daffodil*, runs from Pomona Docks to the Liverpool landing stage and takes some six hours.

The Pomona Docks have a deserted look, though they are still used,

particularly for the 'roll on, roll off' ships where vehicles can drive
directly aboard through the stern. Just beyond the Trafford Road
bridge, the great modern docks begin and are full of life and activity.
Three of them form a group, together with the canal, wide enough for
ships to turn, and the huge dock No. 9 was added in 1905 on the site of
the Manchester racecourse. This is now the main container base, and
by it stands the largest grain elevator in Europe. Three dry docks for
ship repairs lie beyond this on the south side and then comes Mode
Wheel, the highest lock on the canal. The position of the dry docks is
such that a great deal of the water can be drained away to the lower
level beyond the lock. A winking light signal directs the ship into the
larger or the smaller lock, and the entire length may be used or gates
beyond the centre may restrict the size and use less water.

The run past Trafford Park is largely by the oil storage depots,
though other large factories occur and Barton power station stands
close to the swing aqueduct. To the west of this, the old canal line
which used to cross the stone aqueduct is visible on the north side. In
less than a mile the M63 strides across the whole valley at a high level,
and beyond it, on the north side, a depression marks the old course of
the Irwell already cut off by Stickins lock.

Barton locks are very like those at Mode Wheel except that the huge
Davyhulme sewage works lies on the left and makes its presence felt in
the air! Just below the locks, in a field on the left, is a hollow with
stonework which may mark the site of Stickins lock. Hulmes Bridge
and Irlam ferries follow and the Irlam locks are much the same
pattern as before. Just below them is the Irlam viaduct, the first of the
four railway deviation bridges. Beyond this, the Mersey falls over a
weir to enter from the south.

Irlam steelworks on the right is now deserted and its buildings are
demolished. Partington coaling basin appears before the Cadishead
railway deviation bridge. It was constructed with the canal for ships to
bunker at the start of their voyages. Few ships burn coal today, but oil
can be taken on here and coal loaded for export. Beyond the
Cadishead ferry are masonry and brickwork adjoining a hollow on the
south side which appear to be the remains of Owlet's Nest lock. Half a
mile west, the river used to curve south and the eastern end of the

curve is visible before reaching the high Warburton toll bridge. This bridge and the similar one at Warrington were built on the same cantilever principle as the Forth bridge.

The little river Bollin enters from the south at Rixton junction and the Mersey swings off to the right to maintain a separate existence to the estuary. The navigation of this section of the river remained open well into this century. A short distance along its course was Butchersfield cut, which shortened the river by about two miles. The original course wandered southwards in a diamond shape towards Lymm and Statham, and this section is cut by the Ship Canal. The channel is clearly visible by the Lymm golf course, and a number of wooden barges lie sunk in it. Beyond this the M6 motorway crosses the valley in much the same way as the M63. On the north side, between the canal and the river, are the Woolston deposit grounds where dredgings of silt, brought down by the rivers, are deposited.

Latchford locks then take the canal to its final twenty-one-mile pound along the south side of the estuary. The canal first passes Warrington, flowing beneath the railway deviation bridge, the Knutsford road swing bridge and the high-level road bridge. Beyond, and almost beneath the Northwich road swing bridge, is Twenty Steps lock, no longer workable, where the Latchford canal entered from the north. About a quarter of a mile on is another branch on the north side which divides into two. The cut to the north-east, an old loop of the Mersey, served timber yards and warehouses, and that to the north-west linked with the tidal Mersey through Walton lock. This is a barge lock, 150 ft by 30 ft, and is still used.

Beyond the Chester road swing bridge is the last of the railway deviation bridges at Acton Grange, and the canal runs almost straight towards Runcorn, isolating a sort of no-man's-land linked by Moore Lane swing bridge in the centre and Old Quay swing bridge at the western end. Half-way along this are the Randles sluices where the Mersey estuary swings in close to the canal.

The Old Quay Company's wharf, now used as a tugboat base, lies on the south side as the canal reaches Runcorn. The famous transporter bridge has gone, and the canal now passes beneath the new high-level road bridge and the only railway bridge that was built at a sufficiently high level to avoid the need for a deviation. The canal makes its sharpest curve here around the rocky Runcorn promontory and is separated from the narrows of the estuary by a concrete wall.

The eighteenth-century Bridgewater House beyond the curve is now used as offices by the Ship Canal Company. Alongside its gardens the original locks of the Bridgewater canal descended, and the bottom gates of the lowest lock are still visible. The line of the later set of locks can also be made out alongside a row of cottages, though this line is broken by two huge modern sheds. Beneath these, the bottom lock can also be seen.

Saltport is next passed and then British Waterways' Weston Point docks with attractive little hexagonal tollhouses on either side of the entrance and All Saints, the sailors' church, alongside. The docks of Weston Point and Runcorn used to be linked by the Runcorn and Weston canal, now abandoned. Its most southerly lock from the Weaver navigation can still be seen. On the landward side of the ship canal, south of this point, is a line of masonry which looks like the side wall of a lock, with the recesses for the gates visible and the iron pigeonhole ladder in the wall. Similar lock walls are to be seen further up the Weaver navigation, and this would appear to mark the exit to the estuary of the Weaver canal before the ship canal was built. A little farther south, the Weaver sluices are available to empty flood waters into the estuary.

From Weston the canal runs past marshes and more deposit grounds for dredgings and then through the narrower rock channel past Ince and Stanlow where lie the oil refineries. The oil tankers use docks on the north side of the canal, and a great deal of oil is brought by pipe from the large Queen Elizabeth dock at Eastham and from Tranmere, where there are moorings deep enough for the giant tankers which cannot come farther up the estuary.

Ellesmere Port is next reached, with its deep moorings and its base for containers. The entrance to the old canal port is marked by a small lighthouse which used to light the way when ships came up the wide estuary. The basins lie behind, once busy but now silent and abandoned. The top basin with its attractive eighteenth- and early nineteenth-century buildings is being restored by the council in close co-operation with the North Western Museum of Inland Navigation. A variety of significant canal and river commercial craft are to make this their home. There will be repair shops and all necessary workshops and it is intended to reconstruct a nineteenth-century canal port to demonstrate the history of inland navigation.

The canal now passes Mount Manisty, a man-made hill built of material from the excavations, and on the left are piles of tree trunks imported by Bowater's to make paper. Two miles beyond is a wharf with its masting crane. Ships which arrived with masts or funnels too high to pass beneath the bridges could have the tops lifted off and stored until they returned.

Eastham locks finally provide access to the tidal waters and to the deep Eastham channel, which swings in close to the cliffs and woodlands of Eastham ferry. Once the Mersey ferries ran regularly to a little pier and brought thousands of visitors yearly.

So the canal stands today carrying millions of tons of goods yearly to Manchester and to the oil installations and the ports along its length. It was fortunate that it came so late, for otherwise it would have been too small for its present purpose. In cutting out the dock charges at Liverpool and the cost of carrying goods to and from Manchester it altered the industrial scene of the whole region. Today it is adapting itself to the changing times and is in the forefront of containerisation.

Bibliography

1   Aikin, J., *A description of the country from thirty to forty miles round Manchester*, London, 1795.
2   Boucher, C. T. G., *Norwester*, 1954, 1959, 1960 and 1961.
3   Bridgewater Canal, The, *Bi-centenary handbook*, London, 1961.
4   Chaloner, W. H., 'Charles Roe of Macclesfield, 1715–81: an eighteenth century industrialist', *Trans. Lancs. & Ches. Antiq. Soc.*, **62** and **63**, 1953 and 1954.
5   Chaloner, W. H., in *Manchester and its region*, Manchester, 1962.
6   Clowes, P., 'The Peak Forest limestone tramway', *Railway Mag.*, 1963.
7   Corbett, J., *The River Irwell*, Manchester, 1907.
8   De Salis, H. R., *Bradshaw's Canals and navigable rivers of England and Wales*, London, 1904, rep. Newton Abbot, 1969.
9   Dupin, F. P. C., *The commercial power of Great Britain*, London, 1825.
10 Dutens, J. M., *Mémoires sur les travaux publics de l'Angleterre*, Paris, 1819.
11 Egerton, F. H., 'Description of the underground inclined plane, etc.', *Trans. Roy. Soc. Arts.*, **18**, 1800.
12 Farnie, D. A., 'The Manchester Ship Canal, 1894–1913', in *Trade and Transport*, ed. W. H. Chaloner and B. M. Ratcliffe, Manchester, 1977.
13 Fournel, H., and Dyévre, I., *Mémoire sur les canaux souterrains et sur les houillères de Worsley près Manchester*, Paris, 1842.
14 Hadfield, C., *The canal age*, Newton Abbot, 1968.
15 Hadfield, C., and Biddle, G., *The canals of north-west England*, Newton Abbot, 1970.
16 Hanson, H., *The canal boatmen*, Manchester, 1975.
17 Head, G., *A home tour through the manufacturing districts of England in the summer of 1835*, London, 1836, rep. London, 1968.
18 Hogrewe, J. L., *Beschreibung der in England zeit 1759 angelegten und jetzt grössentheils vollendeten schiffbaren kanäle zur innern Gemeinschaft der vornehmsten Handelstädt*, Hanover, 1780.
19 Hollinshead, J., 'On the canal', *Household Words*, 1858.
20 Huerne de Pommeuse, L. F., *Des canaux navigables*, Paris, 1822.

21 Jackman, W. T., *The development of transportation in modern England*, Cambridge, 1916, rep. London, 1966.

22 Jars, G., *Metallurgische reisen zur Untersuchung und Beobachtung de vornehmsten eisen-, stahl-, blech-, und steinkohlen-werke in Deutchsland, Schweden, Norwegen, England und Schotland von jahr 1757 bis 1769*, Berlin, 1777–85.

23 Keaveney, E., and Brown, D. L., *The Ashton Canal*, Manchester, 1974.

24 Leech, B. T., *History of the Manchester Ship Canal*, Manchester, 1907.

25 Lewery, A. J., *Narrow boat painting*, Newton Abbot, 1974.

26 Malet, H., *Bridgewater: the canal duke*, Manchester, 1977.

27 *Manchester and Salford Directories*, Manchester, 1802–19.

28 'The Manchester Ship Canal', *Engineering*, London, 1894.

29 Meteyard, E., *The life of Josiah Wedgwood*, London, 1865.

30 Millward, L., in *The Manchester, Bolton and Bury Canal*, Manchester Education Department, 1975.

31 Mullineux, F., 'The Duke of Bridgewater's canal', *Eccles and District Hist. Soc.*, 1959.

32 Mullineux, F., 'The Duke of Bridgewater's underground canals at Worsley', *Trans. Lancs. & Ches. Antiq. Soc.*, **71**, 1961.

33 Owen, D. E., *Water rallies*, London, 1969.

34 Palmer, J., *Navvies' Notebook*, London, 1968 and 1972.

35 Priestley, J., *Historical account of the navigable rivers, canals and railways of Great Britain*, London, 1831, rep. Newton Abbot, 1969.

36 Prior, M., 'Early canal boat decoration', *Notes and Queries*, new series, **16**, No. 2, 1969.

37 Rimmer, A., *The Cromford and High Peak Railway*, Locomotion Papers, **10**, Lingfield, 1962.

38 Seyd, E. L., *Old Billy, 1760–1822. The world's oldest horse*, Manchester, 1973.

39 Seymour, J., *Voyage into England*, Newton Abbot, 1966.

40 Stoker, R. B., *Sixty years on the western ocean*, Liverpool, 1959.

41 Strickland, W., *Reports on canals, railways, etc.*, Philadelphia, 1826.

42 Thelwall, R. E., *The Andrews and Compstall, their village*, Chester, 1972.

43 Tomlinson, V. I., 'The Manchester, Bolton and Bury Canal Navigation and Railway Company', *Trans. Lancs. & Ches. Antiq. Soc.*, **75–76**, 1965–66.

44 Tomlinson, W., *Byeways of Manchester life, etc.*, Manchester, 1887.

45 Tupling, G. F., in *Manchester and its region*, Manchester, 1962.

46 Ward, J. R., *The finance of canal building in eighteenth century England*, London, 1974.

47 Westall, G., *Inland cruising on the rivers and canals of England and Wales*, London, 1908.

48 Willan, T. S., *River navigation in England, 1600–1750*, London, 1936.

49 Willan, T. S., *The navigation of the River Weaver in the eighteenth century*, Chetham Soc., third series, **3**.

50 Williams, H. L., in *Port of Manchester, 1708—1901*, Manchester, 1901.

Index